Rust for Functional Programmers:

A Hands-on Guide for Mastering Iterators, Closures, and More.

By
Daniel C. Mathews.

TABLE OF CONTENTS

CHAPTER 3: Functions as First-Class Citizens

CHAPTER 4: Mastering Iterators

CHAPTER 5: Closures: Capturing and Computing

CHAPTER 6: Working with Options and Results: Handling Uncertainty

CHAPTER 7: Functional Design Patterns in Rust

CHAPTER 8: Concurrency and Parallelism with Functional Principles

CHAPTER 9: Putting It All Together: Building a Functional Application

CHAPTER 1

SETTING THE STAGE: Functional Programming in Rust

Embracing the Functional Paradigm: A New Way to Think About Code

Functional programming, at its core, is a programming paradigm—a way of thinking about and structuring your code. It emphasizes treating computation as the evaluation of mathematical functions and avoids changing-state and mutable data. This approach can lead to cleaner, more predictable, and easier-to-reason-about code. Let's break down the key concepts that define functional programming:

1. Immutability: The Power of Unchanging Data

Immutability is a fundamental principle in functional programming. It means that once a piece of data is created, it cannot be changed. Think of it like a constant in mathematics – its value is fixed. This might seem restrictive at first, but it brings several significant advantages:

- Predictability: Because data doesn't change after it's created, you can reason about your code more easily. You don't have to worry about a function unexpectedly modifying data somewhere else in your program, leading to subtle bugs. The state of your program becomes much more predictable.
- Thread Safety: In concurrent programming, where multiple threads access and modify shared data, immutability eliminates a major source of bugs: race conditions. Since data can't be changed, there's no need for complex locking mechanisms to protect it. This simplifies concurrent programming significantly.
- Simplified Debugging: When something goes wrong, immutability makes it easier to track down the source of the problem. You know that the data you're working with has a consistent value throughout its lifetime, making it easier to pinpoint where an error occurred.
- Improved Code Readability: Immutability makes code easier to understand because you can clearly see the flow of data transformations without worrying about hidden side effects.

In Rust, immutability is a core concept enforced by the compiler. By default, variables are immutable. You have to explicitly declare a variable as mutable using the mut keyword if you need to change its value. This encourages immutability by default, making it easier to write functional-style code.

2. Pure Functions: The Essence of Predictability

A pure function is a function that has two key properties:

- Deterministic: Given the same input, a pure function will always produce the same output. It doesn't rely on any hidden state or external factors that could influence the result.
- No Side Effects: A pure function does not modify any data outside of its own scope. It doesn't change global variables, write to files, or interact with the external environment in any way that would affect the rest of the program.

These properties make pure functions incredibly predictable and easy to test. Because they always produce the same output for the same input, you can easily write unit tests to verify their behavior. They also make your code more modular and reusable. You can combine pure functions to create more complex logic without worrying about unintended consequences.

Example of a pure function in Rust:

```rust
Rust

fn add(x: i32, y: i32) -> i32 {
    x + y
}
```

This function add is pure because it always returns the same result for the same inputs x and y, and it doesn't have any side effects.

Example of a function with side effects (not pure):

Rust

```
static mut COUNTER: i32 = 0; // Mutable global variable

fn increment_counter(x: i32) -> i32 {
    unsafe {
        COUNTER += x;
        COUNTER
    }
}
```

This function is *not* pure because it modifies the global variable COUNTER (a side effect). Its output depends not only on the input x but also on the current value of COUNTER.

3. Higher-Order Functions: Functions That Operate on Other Functions

Higher-order functions are functions that can either:

- Take other functions as arguments.
- Return functions as results.

This ability to treat functions as first-class citizens is a powerful feature of functional programming. It allows you to create abstractions and write more generic and reusable code. Higher-order functions are essential for implementing many functional programming patterns, such as map, filter, and reduce, which we'll explore in detail later.

Example of a higher-order function in Rust:

Rust

```rust
fn apply_twice(f: fn(i32) -> i32, x: i32) -> i32 {
    let result = f(x);
    f(result)
}

fn square(x: i32) -> i32 {
    x * x
}

fn main() {
    let result = apply_twice(square, 3);
    println!("{}", result); // Output: 81
}
```

In this example, apply_twice is a higher-order function because it takes another function f as an argument. We pass the square function to apply_twice, which then applies square twice to the input 3.

These three concepts – immutability, pure functions, and higher-order functions – are the building blocks of functional programming. By embracing these principles, you can write code that is more robust, predictable, and easier to maintain. In the following chapters, we will explore how these concepts are applied in Rust and how you can use them to write elegant and efficient functional programs.

Rust's Functional Edge: How Ownership, Borrowing, and Types Supercharge Functional Programming

Rust, while not exclusively a functional language, provides a powerful and unique environment for writing functional-style code. Its combination of features, particularly its ownership and borrowing system along with its robust type system, makes it an excellent choice for functional programmers seeking performance, safety, and expressiveness. Let's explore why:

1. Ownership and Borrowing: Enabling Immutability and Fearless Concurrency

As seen in our previous discussion , immutability is a cornerstone of functional programming. Rust's ownership system directly supports this principle. By default, variables are immutable. This aligns perfectly with the functional emphasis on unchanging data. While you can opt into mutability with mut, the language encourages you to think in terms of immutable data structures and transformations.

The borrowing system further enhances the functional experience. It allows you to share access to data without the risks associated with mutable shared state, a common source of bugs in concurrent programming. You can have multiple immutable borrows of a piece of data simultaneously, enabling efficient data sharing without compromising safety. This is crucial for writing concurrent functional programs where you want to operate on shared data without race conditions or data corruption.

Consider how this contrasts with languages that rely on garbage collection and mutable shared state. In those environments, ensuring data consistency in concurrent scenarios often requires complex locking mechanisms, which can introduce performance overhead and increase the risk of deadlocks. Rust's ownership and borrowing system eliminates these concerns, enabling "fearless concurrency" – the ability to write safe and efficient concurrent code without the usual anxieties.

2. The Type System: Enforcing Correctness and Expressing Functional Concepts

Rust's strong, static type system plays a vital role in supporting functional programming. It allows you to express functional concepts clearly and ensures correctness at compile time.

- Algebraic Data Types (ADTs): Rust's enum type allows you to define algebraic data types, which are perfect for representing data structures commonly used in functional programming. For example, you can define an Option type to represent the possibility of a value being present or absent, or a Result type to handle potential errors in a functional way (as discussed in Chapter 6). These types allow for precise data modeling and enable powerful pattern matching, a key feature for functional data manipulation.

- Traits: Rust's trait system allows you to define shared behavior that can be implemented for different types. Traits are particularly useful for working with iterators (Chapter 4). The Iterator trait defines a standard interface for iterating over data, allowing you to write generic functions that can work with any type that implements the Iterator trait. This promotes code reusability and abstraction, which are important in functional programming.

- Higher-Kinded Types (HKTs) (Advanced): While not directly supported in the same way as some other functional languages, Rust's generics and associated types can be used to achieve similar effects to higher-kinded types. This allows for more advanced functional abstractions, like defining generic data structures that can hold other data structures.

- Type Inference: Rust's type inference capabilities reduce the amount of explicit type annotation required, making your code more concise and readable while still maintaining the benefits of a strong type system.

3. Performance: The Power of Zero-Cost Abstractions

Rust is known for its focus on performance. It achieves "zero-cost abstractions," meaning that you can use high-level functional programming techniques without sacrificing performance. Rust compiles down to very efficient machine code, often comparable to C or C++. This makes it a great choice for applications where performance is critical, even when using a functional style.

Rust's lack of a runtime garbage collector is a key factor in its performance. Garbage collection can introduce unpredictable pauses and overhead. Rust's ownership and borrowing system avoids the need for garbage collection, leading to more predictable and consistent performance.

4. Ergonomics and Tooling: A Modern Functional Experience

Rust has a modern and well-designed toolchain, including a powerful package manager (Cargo) and an excellent compiler with helpful error messages. This makes it a pleasure to work with, even when writing complex functional programs.

In summary: Rust's ownership and borrowing system, combined with its powerful type system, creates a unique environment for functional programming. It provides the safety and performance of a systems language while also offering the expressiveness and elegance of a functional language. This combination makes Rust an excellent choice for developers who want to write efficient, reliable, and maintainable code in a functional style.

Setting Up Your Rust Development Environment: A Smooth Start to Your Functional Journey

Before you embark on your journey to master functional programming in Rust, you need to set up your development environment. Fortunately, Rust has a straightforward and well-documented installation process, along with excellent tooling to help you write, build, and manage your projects. This section will guide you through the steps to get your environment up and running, ensuring a smooth start to your Rust development experience.

1. Installing Rust:

The primary tool you'll need is the Rust compiler, rustc, along with the Rust package manager, Cargo. These are bundled together in the Rust toolchain. The easiest way to install the Rust toolchain is using rustup, a command-line tool specifically designed for managing Rust installations.

- Using rustup (Recommended):
    - Visit the official Rust website (https://www.rust-lang.org/tools/install) and follow the instructions for your operating system. You'll typically download and run a script that will install rustup and the latest stable version of the Rust toolchain.

- Once the installation is complete, you can verify it by opening a new terminal window and running the following command:
- <!-- end list -->
- Bash

```
rustc --version
```

-
- This should display the version of the Rust compiler you installed.
- Alternative Installation Methods:
  - Your System's Package Manager: Some operating systems provide Rust packages through their package managers (e.g., apt on Debian/Ubuntu, brew on macOS). While convenient, these packages might not always be the latest version.
  - Building from Source: If you prefer to build from source, you can download the Rust source code and compile it yourself. This is generally recommended for advanced users who need more control over the installation process.

2. Choosing a Code Editor or IDE:

While you can write Rust code in any text editor, using a code editor or IDE with Rust support can significantly enhance your productivity. Here are some popular options:

- Visual Studio Code (VS Code): VS Code is a lightweight and versatile editor with excellent Rust support through the official Rust extension (rust-analyzer). This extension provides features like code completion, syntax highlighting, error checking, and debugging.
- IntelliJ IDEA: IntelliJ IDEA, with the Rust plugin, offers a robust IDE experience for Rust development.[6] It provides advanced features like refactoring, code navigation, and integration with build tools.
- Sublime Text: Sublime Text, with the Rust Enhanced package, is another popular choice for Rust development. It offers a fast and customizable editing experience.
- Vim/Neovim: Vim and Neovim, with the right plugins (e.g., rust.vim), can be powerful environments for Rust development, especially for those who prefer a keyboard-centric workflow.

Ultimately, the best editor or IDE is a matter of personal preference. Experiment with different options and choose the one that best suits your workflow and needs.

3. Managing Projects with Cargo:

Cargo is Rust's build system and package manager. It simplifies building, running, and managing dependencies for your Rust projects. Here's how you can use Cargo to create a new project:

1. Open a terminal window and navigate to the directory where you want to create your project.
2. Run the following command:

<!-- end list -->

Bash

```
cargo new my_functional_project
```

This will create a new directory named my_functional_project with the following structure:

```
my_functional_project/
├── Cargo.toml
└── src/
    └── main.rs
```

- Cargo.toml: This file contains metadata about your project, including its name, version, and dependencies.
- src/main.rs: This is the main source file for your project.

<!-- end list -->

3. To build and run your project, navigate to the my_functional_project directory in your terminal and run:

<!-- end list -->

Bash

```
cargo run
```

Cargo will compile your code and execute the resulting binary, producing the output "Hello, world!" in the terminal.

4. Exploring the Rust Ecosystem:

Beyond the core tools, the Rust ecosystem offers a wealth of libraries (crates) that can be useful for functional programming. You can find these crates on crates.io (https://crates.io/), the official Rust package registry. Cargo makes it easy to add dependencies to your project by simply listing them in the Cargo.toml file.

With your environment set up, you're now ready to dive into the exciting world of functional programming in Rust! Remember, the official Rust documentation (https://www.rust-lang.org/learn) and the Rust book (https://doc.rust-lang.org/book/) are invaluable resources for learning the language and exploring its features.

Your First Functional Program in Rust: "Hello, Functional World!"

Let's dive into writing your first functional program in Rust. We'll create a simple "Hello, Functional World!" program that demonstrates some basic functional concepts. This will help you get familiar with the syntax and structure of a Rust program while introducing you to the functional style.

The Code:

Rust

```rust
fn main() {
    let message = String::from("Hello, Functional World!");
    println!("{}", message);
}
```

Explanation:

- fn main() {... }: This defines the main function, which is the entry point of every Rust program. The code inside the curly braces {} will be executed when you run the program.
- let message = String::from("Hello, Functional World!");: This line declares an immutable variable named

message and assigns it a string value. Remember, immutability is a key principle in functional programming, and Rust enforces it by default.

- println!("{}", message);: This line uses the println! macro to print the value of the message variable to the console.

Functional Aspects:

Even in this simple example, we can see some elements of functional programming at play:

- Immutability: The message variable is immutable, meaning its value cannot be changed after it's assigned. This aligns with the functional principle of avoiding mutable state.
- Pure Function: The main function, in this case, is a pure function. It doesn't have any side effects (it doesn't modify any external state), and it will always produce the same output for the same input (which is no input in this case).

Running the Program:

Save this code as a file named main.rs. Then, open your terminal, navigate to the directory where you saved the file, and run the following command:

Bash

```
cargo run
```

Cargo, Rust's build system and package manager (discussed in Chapter 1), will compile and run your program. You should see the following output in your terminal:

```
Hello, Functional World!
```

Extending the Example:

Let's make this example a bit more functional by introducing a function to create the greeting message:

Rust

```rust
fn create_greeting(name: &str) -> String {
    format!("Hello, {}!", name)
}

fn main() {
    let message = create_greeting("Functional World");
    println!("{}", message);
}
```

In this modified version, we've defined a function create_greeting that takes a name as input and returns a formatted greeting string. This function is also a pure function:

it doesn't have any side effects, and its output depends only on its input.

This example demonstrates the use of functions as first-class citizens in Rust, a key concept in functional programming (Chapter 3). We're passing the string "Functional World" to the create_greeting function, which returns the formatted message.

This simple "Hello, Functional World!" example provides a taste of functional programming in Rust. As you progress through the book, you'll learn how to apply more advanced functional concepts to build complex and powerful applications.

Rust Syntax Essentials: A Functional Perspective

Now that you've dipped your toes into the functional world with a "Hello, Functional World!" example, let's take a closer look at the basic syntax of Rust through a functional lens. We'll explore variables, data types, and control flow, highlighting how they relate to functional programming principles.

1. Variables: Immutability by Default

In Rust, variables are immutable by default. This aligns perfectly with the functional programming emphasis on avoiding mutable state. When you declare a variable using let, you are creating a binding that cannot be changed:

Rust

```rust
let x = 5;
```

This declares an immutable variable x and binds it to the value 5. Any attempt to modify x after this declaration will result in a compile-time error.

If you need to modify a variable, you must explicitly declare it as mutable using the mut keyword:

Rust

```
let mut y = 10;
y = 20; // This is allowed because y is mutable
```

While mutability is sometimes necessary, Rust encourages you to think in terms of immutability first. This helps you write code that is easier to reason about and less prone to errors.

2. Data Types: Building Blocks for Functional Programs

Rust has a rich set of data types that you can use to build your functional programs. Here are some of the essential ones:

Scalar Types: These represent single values.

- Integers: i8, i16, i32, i64, u8, u16, u32, u64 (signed and unsigned with varying bit sizes)
- Floating-point numbers: f32, f64
- Booleans: bool (true or false)
- Characters: char (Unicode characters)

Compound Types: These group multiple values into a single type.

- Tuples: Fixed-size ordered lists of values of potentially different types.

Rust

```rust
let my_tuple: (i32, &str, bool) = (42, "hello", true);
```

- Arrays: Fixed-size ordered lists of values of the same type.

Rust

```rust
let my_array: [i32; 5] = [1,2,3,4,5];
```

String Types:

- String: A growable, heap-allocated UTF-8 encoded string type.
- &str: A string slice, which is a view into a String or a string literal.

Enums (Algebraic Data Types): Enums allow you to define custom types that can represent one of several possible values.

They are particularly useful for modeling data in a functional style. We'll explore them in more detail in Chapter 2.

3. Control Flow: Directing the Flow of Execution

Rust provides several control flow constructs to direct the execution of your program:

- if/else Expressions: Conditional execution based on a boolean condition.

Rust

```rust
if x > 0 {
    println!("x is positive");
} else if x < 0 {
    println!("x is negative");
} else {
    println!("x is zero");
}
```

- match Expressions: Powerful pattern matching for enums and other data types. We'll cover this in detail in Chapter 2.
- Loops: Repeated execution of a block of code.
  - loop: An infinite loop that continues until explicitly terminated with a break statement.
  - while: A loop that continues as long as a condition is true.

- for: A loop that iterates over a collection of values (we'll discuss this further in Chapter 4 when we explore iterators).

Functional Considerations:

While Rust provides mutable variables and loops, functional programming often favors recursion over imperative loops. Recursion involves defining a function that calls itself, and it can be a powerful way to express iterative logic in a more declarative and functional style.

Pattern matching with match expressions is a cornerstone of functional programming in Rust. It allows you to concisely and safely handle different cases based on the structure of your data.

Rust's if/else expressions are actually expressions, not statements. This means they can evaluate to a value, which can be useful for writing functional-style code that avoids mutable state.

This basic syntax review provides a foundation for understanding and writing Rust code from a functional perspective. As you delve deeper into the world of functional programming in Rust, you'll learn how to leverage these language features to create elegant, efficient, and maintainable programs.

CHAPTER 2

Data Structures and Immutability

Ownership and Borrowing: Rust's Foundation for Immutability and Safe Data Management

Rust's ownership and borrowing system is a core feature that sets it apart from many other languages. It's a powerful system that ensures memory safety without the need for garbage collection, and it has significant implications for immutability and functional programming. Let's explore how ownership and borrowing work, and how they relate to the concepts we've discussed in previous discussions.

Ownership: Each Value Has a Unique Owner

At the heart of Rust's memory management is the concept of ownership. In Rust, every value has a single owner at any given time. When the owner goes out of scope, the value is automatically dropped (deallocated). This simple rule has profound consequences:

- No Dangling Pointers: Ownership prevents dangling pointers, a common source of bugs in languages with manual memory management. A dangling pointer is a pointer that points to memory that has been freed. In

Rust, the compiler ensures that a value cannot be used after its owner has gone out of scope, eliminating the possibility of dangling pointers.

- Automatic Memory Management: Ownership eliminates the need for garbage collection, a runtime process that can introduce unpredictable pauses and overhead. Rust's compile-time ownership checks provide deterministic memory management, leading to more predictable and consistent performance.

Borrowing: Sharing Access to Data

While ownership provides a strong foundation for memory safety, it also introduces restrictions on how data can be shared. This is where borrowing comes in. Borrowing allows you to temporarily share access to a value without transferring ownership. There are two types of borrows:

- Immutable Borrows: These allow you to share read-only access to a value. You can have multiple immutable borrows of a value at the same time. This aligns well with the functional programming principle of immutability, as it allows you to share data without the risk of it being modified.
- Mutable Borrows: These allow you to share write access to a value. However, you can only have one mutable borrow of a value at a time. This prevents data races, which can occur when multiple threads try to modify the same data simultaneously.

Borrowing Rules:

The Rust compiler enforces strict rules for borrowing to ensure memory safety:

- You can have either one mutable borrow or multiple immutable borrows, but not both at the same time.
- Borrows must always be valid. The compiler ensures that a borrow cannot outlive the owner of the borrowed value.

Ownership and Immutability: A Perfect Match

Rust's ownership and borrowing system complements immutability in several ways:

- Encourages Immutability: By default, variables are immutable in Rust. This encourages you to think in terms of immutable data structures and transformations, which is a core principle of functional programming.
- Safe Sharing of Immutable Data: Immutable borrows allow you to share read-only access to data without the risk of it being modified. This is essential for writing concurrent functional programs where you want to operate on shared data without race conditions or data corruption.
- Controlled Mutability: While immutability is preferred, sometimes you need to modify data. Rust's mutable borrows provide a controlled way to do this, ensuring

that only one part of your code can modify a value at a time.

Example:

```rust
fn main() {
    let my_string = String::from("hello"); // my_string owns the string

    let my_reference = &my_string; // my_reference immutably borrows the string

    println!("{}", my_reference); // We can use the reference to access the string

    // my_string is still the owner, and we can continue to use it
    println!("{}", my_string);
}
```

In this example, my_string owns the string "hello". my_reference immutably borrows the string, allowing us to access it without taking ownership. Both my_string and my_reference can be used to access the string because my_reference is an immutable borrow.

Implications for Functional Programming:

- Data Ownership and Transformation: Ownership and borrowing provide a clear and safe way to manage data transformations. When you pass data to a function, you can either transfer ownership or lend it immutably or mutably. This allows you to control how the data is used and modified, preventing unintended side effects.
- Concurrency: The borrowing rules ensure that data can be safely shared between threads without the risk of data races. This makes it easier to write concurrent functional programs that are both safe and efficient.
- Functional Data Structures: Ownership and borrowing enable the creation of efficient and safe functional data structures, such as persistent data structures, which provide immutability while allowing efficient updates.

Ownership and Borrowing in Rust: A Beginner-Friendly Guide with Examples

In previous discussions, we discussed the concepts of ownership and borrowing in Rust. Now, let's solidify your understanding with more examples and code snippets.

Ownership: The Foundation

Remember, in Rust, every value has a single owner. When the owner goes out of scope, the value is automatically deallocated. Think of it like a game of hot potato: whoever is holding the potato when the music stops is responsible for cleaning it up.

Example 1: String Ownership

Rust

```
fn main() {
    let s1 = String::from("hello"); // s1 owns the string

    let s2 = s1; // s2 now owns the string (ownership is moved)

    // println!("{}", s1); // This would cause an error because s1
no longer owns the string
    println!("{}", s2); // This is okay because s2 owns the string
}
```

In this example, s1 initially owns the string "hello". When we assign s1 to s2, ownership is *moved* from s1 to s2. This means s1 can no longer be used to access the string.

Borrowing: Sharing is Caring

Borrowing allows you to temporarily share access to a value without transferring ownership. It's like lending someone the potato for a bit, but you still ultimately own it.

Example 2: Immutable Borrowing

Rust

```
fn main() {
```

```
let s1 = String::from("hello");

    let len = calculate_length(&s1); // Pass a reference to s1
(immutable borrow)

    println!("The length of '{}' is {}.", s1, len);
}

fn calculate_length(s: &String) -> usize { // s borrows the
string
    s.len()
}
```

Here, calculate_length takes a reference to a String as input. This is an immutable borrow, meaning the function can read the string but not modify it. s1 retains ownership, so we can still use it after the function call.

Example 3: Mutable Borrowing

Rust

```
fn main() {
    let mut s = String::from("hello");

    change(&mut s);

    println!("{}", s); // Output: "hello, world!"
```

```
}
```

```
fn change(some_string: &mut String) {
    some_string.push_str(", world!");
}
```

In this case, change takes a mutable reference to a String. This allows the function to modify the string. Note that you can only have one mutable borrow at a time.

Example 4: Borrowing Rules

Rust

```
fn main() {
    let mut s = String::from("hello");

    let r1 = &s; // immutable borrow
    let r2 = &s; // another immutable borrow (okay)

    // let r3 = &mut s; // This would cause an error (cannot have
mutable borrow while immutable borrows exist)

    println!("{} and {}", r1, r2); // This is okay

    let r3 = &mut s; // Now okay because r1 and r2 are out of
scope
```

```
    r3.push_str(", world!");
    println!("{}", r3);
}
```

This example demonstrates the borrowing rules. You can have multiple immutable borrows, but you cannot have a mutable borrow while immutable borrows exist.

More Examples & Code to Solidify Your Understanding

- Experiment with passing ownership and borrowing different types (integers, booleans, tuples, etc.) to functions.
- Try creating your own data structures and practice applying ownership and borrowing rules.
- Explore the Rust documentation for more in-depth explanations and examples.

By practicing and experimenting with these concepts, you'll gain a deeper understanding of ownership and borrowing, which are crucial for writing safe and efficient Rust code, especially in a functional style. Remember, these concepts are fundamental to Rust's memory safety guarantees and its ability to prevent common errors like data races and dangling pointers.

Immutable Data Structures in Rust: Tuples, Arrays, and Vectors

In Rust, you have a variety of immutable data structures at your disposal, each with its own strengths and use cases. These data structures provide the foundation for building functional programs where data is treated as immutable values, transformed and passed around without the risk of unexpected modifications. Let's explore some of the core immutable data structures in Rust: tuples, arrays, and vectors.

1. Tuples: Fixed-Size Collections

Tuples are fixed-size ordered collections of values. They can hold elements of different types, making them versatile for representing various kinds of data.

Key Characteristics:

- Fixed Size: Once created, the size of a tuple cannot be changed.
- Heterogeneous Elements: Tuples can hold elements of different data types.
- Accessed by Index: Elements within a tuple are accessed using their index (starting from 0).

Example:

Rust

```
let my_tuple: (i32, &str, bool) = (42, "hello", true);
```

```
println!("The first element is: {}", my_tuple.0); // Accessing
elements by index
```

Use Cases:

- Representing a record with different fields (e.g., a student record with name, ID, and grade).
- Returning multiple values from a function.
- Pattern matching and destructuring (we'll explore this further in the next chapter).

2. Arrays: Fixed-Size Collections of the Same Type

Arrays are similar to tuples, but they can only hold elements of the same data type.

Key Characteristics:

- Fixed Size: Like tuples, the size of an array is fixed at compile time.
- Homogeneous Elements: Arrays can only hold elements of the same data type.
- Accessed by Index: Elements are accessed using their index.

Example:

Rust

```rust
let my_array: [i32; 5] =;

println!("The third element is: {}", my_array);
```

Use Cases:

- Representing a fixed collection of values of the same type (e.g., coordinates in a 3D space).
- Implementing algorithms that require fixed-size data structures.

3. Vectors: Dynamically Sized Collections

Vectors are dynamically sized collections that can grow or shrink as needed. They are similar to arrays, but their size is not fixed at compile time.

Key Characteristics:

- Dynamic Size: Vectors can grow or shrink as needed.
- Homogeneous Elements: Vectors can only hold elements of the same data type.
- Accessed by Index: Elements are accessed using their index.

Example:

Rust

```rust
let mut my_vector: Vec<i32> = Vec::new(); // Creating an empty vector

my_vector.push(1);
my_vector.push(2);
my_vector.push(3);

println!("The second element is: {}", my_vector);
```

Use Cases:

- Storing a collection of data where the size is not known beforehand (e.g., a list of user inputs).
- Implementing data structures that require dynamic resizing (e.g., a stack or a queue).

Immutability and These Data Structures

By default, all these data structures (tuple, array and vector) are immutable in Rust. This means that once you create them, you cannot change their elements. This aligns perfectly with the principles of functional programming, where data is treated as immutable values.

Example of Immutability:

Rust

```rust
let my_tuple = (1, 2, 3);
```

// my_tuple.0 = 4; // This would cause an error because tuples are immutable

Mutability with mut

If you need to modify the elements of a vector, you can declare it as mutable using the mut keyword. However, this is generally discouraged in functional programming, as immutability provides many benefits like predictability and thread safety.

Example of Mutability with Vectors:

Rust

```
let mut my_vector = vec!;

my_vector = 4; // This is allowed because my_vector is mutable
```

Choosing the Right Data Structure

The choice of which data structure to use depends on your specific needs:

- If you need a fixed-size collection of elements of different types, use a tuple.
- If you need a fixed-size collection of elements of the same type, use an array.

- If you need a dynamically sized collection of elements of the same type, use a vector.

By understanding the characteristics and use cases of these data structures, you can effectively leverage them to build robust and efficient functional programs in Rust. Remember, immutability is a key principle in functional programming, and these data structures provide the foundation for working with immutable data in Rust.

Structs and Enums: Building Blocks for Functional Data in Rust

In Rust, structs and enums are powerful tools for defining custom data types. They provide the foundation for creating complex data structures that can represent a wide range of information in a clear and organized way. With a focus on immutability, a core principle in functional programming, let's explore how structs and enums can be used to model data effectively.

Structs: Organizing Data with Named Fields

Structs allow you to group related data elements together, giving each element a meaningful name. This makes your code more readable and easier to understand.

Key characteristics:

- Named fields: Each data element in a struct is associated with a name, making it clear what the data represents.

- Flexible data types: Structs can hold data of various types, including other structs and enums.
- Immutability by default: Like other data structures in Rust, structs are immutable by default. This means that once you create a struct instance, you cannot modify its fields unless you explicitly declare it as mutable.

Example:

```Rust
struct User {
    username: String,
    email: String,
    active: bool,
}

fn main() {
    let user = User {
        username: String::from("johndoe"),
        email: String::from("john.doe@example.com"),
        active: true,
    };

    println!("Username: {}", user.username); // Accessing fields
using dot notation
}
```

Use cases:

- Representing complex entities with multiple attributes (e.g., a user, a product, a book).
- Organizing data in a hierarchical manner (e.g., a tree structure).
- Creating custom data types that are tailored to your specific needs.

Enums: Representing Multiple Possibilities

Enums, short for enumerations, allow you to define a type that can be one of several named values. This is particularly useful for representing situations where a variable can have a limited set of possible states.

Key characteristics:

- Named variants: Each possible value of an enum is given a descriptive name.
- Data associated with variants: Enums can optionally hold data within each variant.
- Exhaustive matching: The compiler ensures that you handle all possible variants of an enum when using pattern matching (we'll explore this further in the next section).

Example:

Rust

```
enum TrafficLight {
    Red,
```

```
    Yellow,
    Green,
}

fn main() {
    let light = TrafficLight::Yellow;

    //... code to handle the traffic light state...
}
```

Use cases:

- Representing a state machine (e.g., the state of a network connection).
- Modeling data that can have different forms (e.g., a shape that can be a circle, square, or triangle).
- Handling errors in a structured way (e.g., using a Result enum to represent success or failure).

Immutability with Structs and Enums

As mentioned earlier, both structs and enums are immutable by default in Rust. This means that once you create an instance of a struct or assign a value to an enum variable, you cannot modify its fields or variants unless you explicitly declare it as mutable.

Example:

Rust

```rust
struct Point {
    x: i32,
    y: i32,
}

fn main() {
    let point = Point { x: 10, y: 20 };

    // point.x = 30; // This would cause an error because point is immutable
}
```

Mutability with mut

If you need to modify the fields of a struct or the value of an enum variable, you can declare it as mutable using the mut keyword. However, this is generally discouraged in functional programming, as immutability provides many benefits like predictability and thread safety.

Example:

Rust

```rust
struct Counter {
    count: i32,
}
```

```
fn main() {
    let mut counter = Counter { count: 0 };

    counter.count += 1; // This is allowed because counter is
mutable
}
```

Choosing Between Structs and Enums

The choice between using a struct or an enum depends on the nature of the data you want to represent:

- If you need to represent data with named fields, use a struct.
- If you need to represent a type that can be one of several named values, use an enum.

By understanding the characteristics and use cases of structs and enums, you can effectively leverage them to model data in your functional Rust programs. Remember, immutability is a key principle in functional programming, and these data structures provide the foundation for working with immutable data in Rust.

Pattern Matching and Destructuring: Elegant Data Handling in Rust

Pattern matching and destructuring are powerful tools in Rust that allow you to concisely and safely work with data. They are particularly well-suited for functional programming, where data is often immutable and structured in complex ways. Let's explore these concepts in detail and see how they can enhance your functional programming experience in Rust.

Pattern Matching: Conditional Logic with Data Structures

Pattern matching is a powerful construct that allows you to compare a value against a series of patterns and execute different code blocks based on which pattern matches. It's like a sophisticated switch statement that can work with various data types, including enums, structs, tuples, and even primitive types.

Key benefits:

- Conciseness: Pattern matching can often express complex conditional logic more concisely than traditional if/else chains.
- Safety: The compiler ensures that you handle all possible cases when matching against enums, preventing runtime errors due to unhandled variants.
- Expressiveness: Pattern matching allows you to clearly express the intent of your code by directly matching against the structure of your data.

Example with Enums:

Rust

```rust
enum Shape {
    Circle(f64), // Circle with radius
    Rectangle(f64, f64), // Rectangle with width and height
}

fn calculate_area(shape: Shape) -> f64 {
    match shape {
        Shape::Circle(radius) => std::f64::consts::PI * radius *
radius,
        Shape::Rectangle(width, height) => width * height,
    }
}

fn main() {
    let circle = Shape::Circle(5.0);
    let rectangle = Shape::Rectangle(10.0, 5.0);

    println!("Circle area: {}", calculate_area(circle));
    println!("Rectangle area: {}", calculate_area(rectangle));
}
```

In this example, the match expression checks the value of shape against the patterns Shape::Circle(radius) and Shape::Rectangle(width, height). If the shape is a circle, it binds the radius to the variable radius and calculates the area accordingly. If it's a rectangle, it binds the width and height and calculates the area.

Example with Structs:

Rust

```rust
struct Point {
    x: i32,
    y: i32,
}

fn print_point(point: Point) {
    match point {
        Point { x, y } => println!("Point is at ({}, {})", x, y),
    }
}
```

Here, the match expression destructures the Point struct and binds its fields x and y to variables of the same name.

Destructuring: Breaking Down Data Structures

Destructuring is the process of breaking down a complex data structure into its individual components. This is often used in conjunction with pattern matching to extract values from structs, tuples, and enums.

Key benefits:

- Clarity: Destructuring makes it clear which parts of a data structure you are interested in.

- Conciseness: It avoids the need to repeatedly access fields using dot notation or index access.
- Immutability: Destructuring allows you to extract values from immutable data structures without modifying the original structure.

Example with Tuples:

Rust

```rust
fn print_tuple(my_tuple: (i32, &str)) {
    let (number, text) = my_tuple; // Destructuring the tuple
    println!("Number: {}, Text: {}", number, text);
}
```

In this example, the let (number, text) = my_tuple; line destructures the tuple my_tuple into its individual components, binding the first element to number and the second to text.

Example with Structs:

Rust

```rust
struct User {
    username: String,
    email: String,
}

fn print_user(user: User) {
```

```rust
    let User { username, email } = user; // Destructuring the
struct
    println!("Username: {}, Email: {}", username, email);
}
```

Here, the let User { username, email } = user; line destructures the User struct and binds its fields username and email to variables of the same name.

Combining Pattern Matching and Destructuring

Pattern matching and destructuring often work together to provide elegant solutions for data manipulation. You can use pattern matching to check for specific conditions within a data structure and then use destructuring to extract the relevant values.

Example:

Rust

```rust
enum Message {
    Quit,
    Move { x: i32, y: i32 },
    Write(String),
}

fn process_message(msg: Message) {
    match msg {
```

```
    Message::Quit => println!("Quitting..."),
     Message::Move { x, y } => println!("Moving to ({}, {})",
x, y),
     Message::Write(text) => println!("Writing: {}", text),
   }
}
```

In this example, the match expression checks the type of the Message enum. If it's a Move message, it destructures the x and y fields. If it's a Write message, it extracts the text field.

Functional Programming Applications

Pattern matching and destructuring are invaluable tools for functional programming in Rust. They allow you to work with immutable data structures in a safe and expressive way. By leveraging these features, you can write code that is more concise, readable, and maintainable.

- Data Transformation: You can use pattern matching and destructuring to transform data from one form to another, extracting and manipulating values as needed.
- Conditional Logic: Pattern matching provides a powerful way to express complex conditional logic based on the structure of your data.
- Error Handling: Enums like Result can be effectively handled using pattern matching to distinguish between success and failure cases.

- Function Composition: Destructuring can be used to break down complex function arguments into simpler components, making it easier to compose functions together.

Building and Operating on Immutable Data Structures in Rust: Practical Examples

In Rust, immutability is a cornerstone of functional programming, providing predictability, thread safety, and easier reasoning about code. Building and working with immutable data structures is a key skill for writing robust and maintainable functional programs. Let's explore some practical examples of how to create and manipulate immutable data structures in Rust, leveraging the concepts we've covered in previous chapters.

Example 1: Creating an Immutable User Record

Let's say we want to represent a user with attributes like name, email, and active status. We can use a struct to define this data structure, ensuring that once a user is created, their information cannot be changed.

Rust

```rust
struct User {
    username: String,
    email: String,
    active: bool,
```

```
}

fn main() {
    let user = User {
        username: String::from("johndoe"),
        email: String::from("john.doe@example.com"),
        active: true,
    };

    // user.email = String::from("jane.doe@example.com"); //
This would cause an error because user is immutable

    println!("User: {}", user.username);
}
```

In this example, the User struct represents an immutable user record. Once the user instance is created, its fields cannot be modified. This ensures that the user data remains consistent throughout its lifetime.

Example 2: Transforming Data with Immutable Vectors

Vectors, while dynamically sized, can also be immutable. Let's say we have a vector of numbers and want to double each number without modifying the original vector. We can use the map adapter (discussed in Chapter 4) to create a new vector with the transformed values.

Rust

```rust
fn main() {
    let numbers = vec!;

    let doubled_numbers: Vec<i32> = numbers.iter().map(|x| x * 2).collect();

    println!("Original numbers: {:?}", numbers);
    println!("Doubled numbers: {:?}", doubled_numbers);
}
```

In this example, numbers is an immutable vector. The map adapter creates a new iterator that doubles each number, and collect gathers the results into a new vector doubled_numbers. The original numbers vector remains unchanged.

Example 3: Working with Immutable Linked Lists

Linked lists are a common data structure in functional programming. Let's define a simple immutable linked list and perform some operations on it.

Rust

```rust
enum List {
    Cons(i32, Box<List>),
    Nil,
}

use List::{Cons, Nil};
```

```rust
fn main() {
    let list = Cons(1, Box::new(Cons(2, Box::new(Cons(3, Box::new(Nil))))));

    let length = list_length(&list);
    println!("Length of the list: {}", length);

    let sum = list_sum(&list);
    println!("Sum of the list: {}", sum);
}

fn list_length(list: &List) -> i32 {
    match list {
        Cons(_, next) => 1 + list_length(next),
        Nil => 0,
    }
}

fn list_sum(list: &List) -> i32 {
    match list {
        Cons(value, next) => value + list_sum(next),
        Nil => 0,
    }
}
```

In this example, List is an enum representing an immutable linked list. The list_length and list_sum functions demonstrate how to recursively traverse and perform operations on the list without modifying it.

Example 4: Building a Tree with Immutable Structs

Trees are another fundamental data structure in functional programming. Let's create a simple binary tree using immutable structs.

Rust

```rust
struct Node {
    value: i32,
    left: Option<Box<Node>>,
    right: Option<Box<Node>>,
}

fn main() {
    let tree = Node {
        value: 1,
        left: Some(Box::new(Node {
            value: 2,
            left: None,
            right: None,
        })),
        right: Some(Box::new(Node {
            value: 3,
            left: None,
            right: None,
        })),
    };

    //... operations on the tree...
}
```

In this example, Node represents a node in the binary tree. The tree instance is an immutable tree structure. You can perform various operations on this tree, such as calculating its height, searching for a specific value, or traversing it in different orders, all without modifying the original tree structure.

These examples demonstrate how to build and work with immutable data structures in Rust. By embracing immutability, you can write functional programs that are more predictable, easier to reason about, and less prone to errors. Remember, immutability is a key principle in functional programming, and these examples showcase how to apply it effectively in Rust.

CHAPTER 3

Functions as First-Class Citizens

Functions in Rust: The Building Blocks of Functional Programming

In Rust, functions are fundamental building blocks for organizing and structuring code. They encapsulate reusable logic, promote modularity, and play a crucial role in enabling functional programming paradigms. Let's delve into the details of defining and using functions in Rust, highlighting their significance in the context of functional programming.

Defining Functions: Structure and Syntax

Functions in Rust are defined using the fn keyword, followed by the function name, parentheses for parameters, and an optional return type. The code block within curly braces {} constitutes the function body.

Rust

```
fn greet(name: &str) -> String {
    format!("Hello, {}!", name)
}
```

In this example, greet is the function name, name is a parameter of type &str (string slice), and -> String indicates that the function returns a String value. The function body constructs a greeting message using the format! macro.

Parameters and Arguments: Passing Data to Functions

Functions can accept parameters, which act as placeholders for values that are passed to the function when it's called. These passed values are called arguments.

Rust

```
fn add(x: i32, y: i32) -> i32 {
    x + y
}

fn main() {
    let result = add(5, 3); // Calling the function with arguments
5 and 3
    println!("Result: {}", result); // Output: 8
}
```

In this example, add takes two parameters x and y of type i32. When called with arguments 5 and 3, these values are bound to x and y respectively within the function body.

Return Values: Output from Functions

Functions can optionally return a value using the return keyword or by simply placing an expression at the end of the function body without a semicolon.

Rust

```rust
fn square(x: i32) -> i32 {
    x * x // Implicit return
}

fn main() {
    let squared = square(4);
    println!("Squared: {}", squared); // Output: 16
}
```

In this example, square returns the square of its input parameter x. The expression x * x is implicitly returned as the function's result.

Function Signatures: Unique Identifiers

A function's signature consists of its name, parameters, and return type. This signature uniquely identifies the function and distinguishes it from other functions.

Rust

```rust
fn foo(x: i32) -> i32 {... }
fn foo(x: &str) {... } // Different signature due to parameter type
fn foo() -> String {... } // Different signature due to return type
```

These are all distinct functions with different signatures, even though they share the same name.

Function Calls: Executing the Code

Calling a function executes the code within its body. You call a function by using its name followed by parentheses containing the arguments.

Rust

```
let greeting = greet("Alice"); // Calling the greet function
println!("{}", greeting); // Output: Hello, Alice!
```

Functions in Functional Programming

Functions play a central role in functional programming. They are treated as first-class citizens, meaning they can be passed as arguments to other functions, returned from functions, and stored in variables. This enables powerful functional programming techniques like higher-order functions and closures, which we'll explore in later chapters.

Pure Functions: Predictability and Testability

Pure functions are functions that have no side effects and always produce the same output for the same input. They are essential for writing reliable and testable functional code.

Rust

```rust
fn pure_add(x: i32, y: i32) -> i32 {
    x + y // No side effects, deterministic output
}
```

Function Composition: Combining Functions

Function composition is the process of combining multiple functions to create new functions. This allows you to build complex logic from simpler, reusable components.

Rust

```rust
fn double(x: i32) -> i32 {
    x * 2
}

fn square(x: i32) -> i32 {
    x * x
}

fn main() {
    let result = square(double(3)); // Function composition
    println!("Result: {}", result); // Output: 36
}
```

In this example, square(double(3)) effectively composes the double and square functions, first doubling 3 and then squaring the result.

Function Types and Higher-Order Functions in Rust: Embracing Functional Paradigms

Functions are not just blocks of code; they are first-class citizens, meaning they can be treated like any other value. This opens up powerful possibilities for functional programming, enabling techniques like higher-order functions that significantly enhance code expressiveness and reusability. Let's explore function types and higher-order functions in detail, understanding their role in building sophisticated functional programs in Rust.

Function Types: Representing Functions as Values

Every function in Rust has a specific type, just like variables. This type, known as the function type, captures the function's signature, including its parameters and return type.

Rust

```rust
fn add(x: i32, y: i32) -> i32 {
    x + y
}


let add_fn: fn(i32, i32) -> i32 = add; // Assigning the function
to a variable
```

In this example, add_fn is a variable of type fn(i32, i32) -> i32, which represents the type of the add function. This type signifies that the function takes two i32 parameters and returns an i32 value.

Higher-Order Functions: Functions that Operate on Functions

Higher-order functions are functions that take other functions as arguments or return functions as results. This ability to manipulate functions as values unlocks powerful functional programming patterns.

Taking Functions as Arguments:

```rust
Rust

fn apply(f: fn(i32) -> i32, x: i32) -> i32 {
    f(x)
}


fn square(x: i32) -> i32 {
    x * x
}


fn main() {
    let result = apply(square, 5); // Passing the square function
as an argument
    println!("Result: {}", result); // Output: 25
}
```

In this example, apply is a higher-order function that takes a function f as an argument. It applies the given function to the input x and returns the result.

Returning Functions from Functions:

Rust

```
fn make_multiplier(factor: i32) -> fn(i32) -> i32 {
    fn multiplier(x: i32) -> i32 {
        x * factor
    }
    multiplier // Returning the multiplier function
}

fn main() {
    let double = make_multiplier(2); // Creating a function that doubles its input
    let triple = make_multiplier(3); // Creating a function that triples its input

    println!("Double: {}", double(5)); // Output: 10
    println!("Triple: {}", triple(5)); // Output: 15
}
```

In this example, make_multiplier is a higher-order function that returns a new function. The returned function multiplies its input by the factor specified when creating the multiplier.

Benefits of Higher-Order Functions

- Abstraction and Code Reusability: Higher-order functions allow you to abstract common patterns of computation, making your code more reusable and easier to understand.
- Flexibility and Customization: By passing functions as arguments, you can customize the behavior of higher-order functions without modifying their core logic.
- Function Composition: Higher-order functions enable function composition, allowing you to combine simple functions to create more complex ones.

Examples in Functional Programming

Higher-order functions are prevalent in functional programming paradigms. Common examples include:

- Map: Applies a function to each element of a collection, returning a new collection with the transformed elements (will be discussed in Chapter 4).
- Filter: Selects elements from a collection based on a predicate function, returning a new collection with only the elements that satisfy the predicate.
- Fold (Reduce): Combines the elements of a collection into a single value by repeatedly applying a function.

Closures: Anonymous Functions with Captured Context

Closures are anonymous functions that can capture variables from their surrounding scope. They are often used in conjunction with higher-order functions to provide customized behavior.

Rust

```
fn main() {
    let factor = 3;
    let multiplier = |x| x * factor; // Closure capturing the factor variable

    println!("Result: {}", multiplier(5)); // Output: 15
}
```

In this example, multiplier is a closure that captures the factor variable from its surrounding scope.

Function Pointers: Raw Function Values

Function pointers are raw pointers to functions. They are less common than function types and closures but can be useful in certain scenarios, such as interacting with external libraries or low-level code.

Rust

```
fn add(x: i32, y: i32) -> i32 {
    x + y
}

let add_ptr: fn(i32, i32) -> i32 = add; // Function pointer
```

```
let result = (add_ptr)(5, 3); // Calling the function through the
pointer
```

By understanding function types, higher-order functions, closures, and function pointers, you can unlock the full potential of functional programming in Rust. These concepts enable you to write code that is more expressive, reusable, and adaptable to various scenarios.

Passing Functions as Arguments and Returning Functions from Functions: Embracing Higher-Order Functions in Rust

In Rust, functions are first-class citizens, meaning they can be treated like any other value. This powerful feature allows you to pass functions as arguments to other functions and even return functions from functions. These techniques, known as higher-order functions, unlock a new level of expressiveness and flexibility in your code, enabling you to write more modular, reusable, and functional programs. Let's explore these concepts in detail.

Passing Functions as Arguments

Passing a function as an argument to another function allows you to customize the behavior of the receiving function. This is particularly useful when you want to apply a specific operation to a set of data, but you don't want to hardcode the operation within the function itself.

Example:

Rust

```rust
fn apply_operation(f: fn(i32) -> i32, x: i32) -> i32 {
    f(x)
}

fn square(x: i32) -> i32 {
    x * x
}

fn double(x: i32) -> i32 {
    x * 2
}

fn main() {
    let result1 = apply_operation(square, 5); // Passing the square function
    println!("Square: {}", result1); // Output: 25

    let result2 = apply_operation(double, 5); // Passing the double function
    println!("Double: {}", result2); // Output: 10
}
```

In this example, apply_operation is a higher-order function that takes a function f as an argument. This function f is expected to take an i32 as input and return an i32 as output. The apply_operation function then applies the given function f to the input x and returns the result.

This allows you to reuse the apply_operation function with different operations, simply by passing different functions as arguments. This promotes code reusability and avoids code duplication.

Returning Functions from Functions

Returning a function from another function allows you to create customized functions on the fly. This can be useful for creating functions that have some internal state or configuration that is determined at runtime.

Example:

Rust

```
fn make_multiplier(factor: i32) -> fn(i32) -> i32 {
    fn multiplier(x: i32) -> i32 {
      x * factor
    }
    multiplier
}

fn main() {
    let double = make_multiplier(2); // Creating a function that doubles its input
    let triple = make_multiplier(3); // Creating a function that triples its input
```

```
    println!("Double: {}", double(5)); // Output: 10
    println!("Triple: {}", triple(5)); // Output: 15
}
```

In this example, make_multiplier is a higher-order function that returns a new function. The returned function, multiplier, takes an i32 as input and multiplies it by the factor that was passed to make_multiplier. This allows you to create customized multiplier functions with different factors.

Benefits of Passing and Returning Functions

- Flexibility and Customization: Higher-order functions allow you to customize the behavior of functions without modifying their core logic.
- Code Reusability: By passing and returning functions, you can create more generic and reusable code that can be adapted to different situations.
- Abstraction: Higher-order functions enable you to abstract common patterns of computation, making your code more concise and easier to understand.
- Function Composition: Passing and returning functions facilitates function composition, allowing you to combine simple functions to create more complex ones.

Examples in Functional Programming

Passing and returning functions are fundamental techniques in functional programming. They are used extensively in various functional programming paradigms and patterns, such as:

- Currying: Transforming a function that takes multiple arguments into a sequence of functions that each take a single argument.
- Partial Application: Fixing a subset of the arguments of a function to create a new function with fewer arguments.
- Function Composition: Combining multiple functions to create new functions.
- Higher-Order Functions in Collections: Functions like map, filter, and fold (will be discussed in Chapter 4) take functions as arguments to operate on collections.

Implementing Common Functional Patterns with Basic Functions in Rust

In Rust, you can implement common functional patterns like map, filter, and reduce using basic functions, even without relying on the built-in Iterator trait (which we'll explore in Chapter 4). This approach helps you understand the underlying principles of these patterns and how they can be implemented using fundamental functional programming concepts.

Map: Transforming Data

The map pattern applies a function to each element of a collection, producing a new collection with the transformed elements.

Example:

Rust

```rust
fn square(x: i32) -> i32 {

  x * x

}

fn map(f: fn(i32) -> i32, v: Vec<i32>) -> Vec<i32> {

   let mut result = Vec::new();

   for x in v {

      result.push(f(x));

   }

   result

}

fn main() {

   let numbers = vec!;

   let squared_numbers = map(square, numbers);

   println!("{:?}", squared_numbers); // Output:
```

```
}
```

In this example, map takes a function f and a vector v as input. It creates a new vector result and iterates over the elements of v, applying the function f to each element and pushing the result into result.

Filter: Selecting Data

The filter pattern selects elements from a collection based on a predicate function, producing a new collection containing only the elements that satisfy the predicate.

Example:

Rust

```rust
fn is_even(x: i32) -> bool {

    x % 2 == 0

}

fn filter(f: fn(i32) -> bool, v: Vec<i32>) -> Vec<i32> {

    let mut result = Vec::new();

    for x in v {

        if f(x) {

            result.push(x);
```

```rust
        }

    }

    result

}

fn main() {

    let numbers = vec!;

    let even_numbers = filter(is_even, numbers);

    println!("{:?}", even_numbers); // Output:

}
```

In this example, filter takes a predicate function f and a vector v as input. It creates a new vector result and iterates over the elements of v, adding an element to result only if the predicate function f returns true for that element.

Reduce: Combining Data

The reduce pattern (also known as fold) combines the elements of a collection into a single value by repeatedly applying a function.

Example:

Rust

```rust
fn add(x: i32, y: i32) -> i32 {

    x + y

}


fn reduce(f: fn(i32, i32) -> i32, initial: i32, v: Vec<i32>) -> i32
{

    let mut result = initial;

    for x in v {

        result = f(result, x);

    }

    result

}

fn main() {

    let numbers = vec!;

    let sum = reduce(add, 0, numbers);

    println!("{}", sum); // Output: 15

}
```

In this example, reduce takes a function f, an initial value initial, and a vector v as input. It initializes a variable result with the initial value and iterates over the elements of v, applying the function f to the current result and the current element, updating result with the new value.

These examples demonstrate how to implement common functional patterns using basic functions in Rust. By understanding these implementations, you gain a deeper appreciation for the power and flexibility of functional programming concepts. In later chapters, we'll explore how these patterns are implemented using the Iterator trait, which provides a more concise and efficient way to work with collections in a functional style.

CHAPTER 4

Mastering Iterators

The Iterator Trait: A Cornerstone of Functional Programming in Rust

In Rust, the Iterator trait is a fundamental abstraction that provides a powerful and elegant way to work with collections of data. It's a cornerstone of functional programming in Rust, enabling you to process sequences of elements in a declarative and composable manner. Let's explore the Iterator trait in detail, understanding its significance and how it empowers you to write efficient and expressive functional code.

What is the Iterator Trait?

The Iterator trait defines a common interface for iterating over elements in a collection. Any type that implements the Iterator trait can be used to produce a sequence of values. This abstraction allows you to write generic code that can work with various collection types, such as vectors, arrays, hash maps, and even custom data structures.

The next Method: The Heart of Iteration

At the core of the Iterator trait is the next method. This method produces the next item in the sequence, or None if the sequence is exhausted.

Rust

```
pub trait Iterator {
    type Item;
    fn next(&mut self) -> Option<Self::Item>;
    // ... other methods ...
}
```

This code snippet shows the basic structure of the Iterator trait. The Item associated type defines the type of elements produced by the iterator. The next method takes a mutable reference to self and returns an Option<Self::Item>, representing either the next item in the sequence or None if there are no more items.

Iterating with for Loops

The most common way to use an iterator is with a for loop. The for loop automatically calls the next method on the iterator until None is returned.

Rust

```
fn main() {
    let numbers = vec!;
    for number in numbers.iter() { // Creating an iterator and
iterating with a for loop
```

```
        println!("{}", number);
    }
}
```

In this example, numbers.iter() creates an iterator over the numbers vector. The for loop then consumes the iterator, printing each number in the sequence.

Iterator Adapters: Chaining Operations

One of the most powerful features of iterators is the ability to chain operations together using iterator adapters. Adapters are methods that transform an iterator into another iterator, allowing you to perform complex data manipulations in a concise and readable way.

Example:

Rust

```
fn main() {
    let numbers = vec!;
    let doubled_even_numbers: Vec<i32> = numbers
        .iter()
        .filter(|x| *x % 2 == 0) // Filter for even numbers
        .map(|x| x * 2) // Double each even number
        .collect(); // Collect the results into a new vector

    println!("{:?}", doubled_even_numbers); // Output:
}
```

In this example, we chain the filter and map adapters to first select even numbers and then double them. The collect method gathers the final results into a new vector.

Common Iterator Adapters

The Iterator trait provides a rich set of adapters for various data transformations, including:

- map: Applies a function to each element.
- filter: Selects elements based on a predicate.
- fold: Combines elements into a single value.
- zip: Combines two iterators into a single iterator of pairs.
- enumerate: Adds a counter to each element.
- skip: Skips the first n elements.
- take: Takes the first n elements.

Importance in Functional Programming

The Iterator trait is crucial for functional programming in Rust for several reasons:

- Composability: Iterator adapters allow you to compose complex data transformations from simpler operations, promoting code reusability and modularity.
- Laziness: Iterators are lazy, meaning they only compute values when they are needed. This can improve performance by avoiding unnecessary computations.

- Abstraction: The Iterator trait provides a common interface for working with various collection types, enabling you to write generic code that is not tied to specific data structures.
- Immutability: Iterators often operate on immutable data, aligning with the functional programming principle of avoiding mutable state.

Beyond the Basics

The Iterator trait offers even more advanced features, such as:

- Custom Iterators: You can implement the Iterator trait for your own data structures, enabling them to be used with iterator adapters and for loops.
- Parallel Iterators: The rayon crate provides parallel iterators, allowing you to process elements concurrently for improved performance.
- Infinite Iterators: You can create iterators that produce an infinite sequence of values, useful for generating sequences or modeling streams of data.

By understanding and leveraging the Iterator trait, you can unlock the full potential of functional programming in Rust. It provides a powerful and elegant way to work with collections of data, enabling you to write code that is expressive, efficient, and maintainable.

Creating and Using Iterators with Various Data Structures in Rust

Iterators in Rust provide a powerful and flexible way to work with collections of data. They allow you to process elements sequentially without having to worry about the underlying implementation details of the collection. In this section, we'll explore how to create and use iterators with various data structures in Rust, showcasing the versatility and expressiveness of this approach.

Iterating over Vectors

Vectors are one of the most common data structures in Rust, and they provide a straightforward way to create iterators. The iter method on a vector returns an iterator that yields immutable references to each element.

Rust

```rust
fn main() {
    let numbers = vec!;

    for number in numbers.iter() {
        println!("{}", number);
    }
}
```

In this example, numbers.iter() creates an iterator over the numbers vector. The for loop then consumes the iterator, printing each number in the sequence.

If you need to modify the elements of the vector while iterating, you can use the iter_mut method, which yields mutable references.

Rust

```rust
fn main() {
    let mut numbers = vec!;

    for number in numbers.iter_mut() {
        *number *= 2; // Double each number
    }

    println!("{:?}", numbers); // Output:
}
```

Iterating over Arrays

Arrays, like vectors, also provide methods for creating iterators. The iter and iter_mut methods work similarly to their vector counterparts, yielding immutable and mutable references to the array elements, respectively.

Rust

```rust
fn main() {
    let numbers =;

    for number in numbers.iter() {
        println!("{}", number);
```

```
    }
}
```

Iterating over Slices

Slices are views into a contiguous sequence of elements in a collection. They can be created from vectors, arrays, and even string slices. You can create iterators over slices using the iter and iter_mut methods, just like with vectors and arrays.

```
fn main() {
    let numbers =;
    let slice = &numbers[1..4]; // Create a slice from the array

    for number in slice.iter() {
        println!("{}", number);
    }
}
```

Iterating over Strings

Strings in Rust provide various ways to create iterators. The chars method returns an iterator over the individual characters of the string.

```rust
fn main() {
    let message = "Hello, world!";

    for ch in message.chars() {
        println!("{}", ch);
    }
}
```

You can also iterate over the bytes of a string using the bytes method, or over the lines of a multi-line string using the lines method.

Iterating over Hash Maps

Hash maps provide iterators for traversing their key-value pairs. The iter method returns an iterator over immutable references to the key-value pairs.

Rust

```rust
use std::collections::HashMap;

fn main() {
    let mut scores = HashMap::new();
    scores.insert("Alice", 10);
    scores.insert("Bob", 20);

    for (key, value) in scores.iter() {
        println!("{}: {}", key, value);
    }
```

```
}
```

If you need to modify the values in the hash map while iterating, you can use the iter_mut method, which yields mutable references to the values.

Creating Custom Iterators

You can also create your own custom iterators by implementing the Iterator trait for your own data structures. This allows you to integrate your custom data structures seamlessly with Rust's iterator ecosystem.

Rust

```rust
struct Counter {
    count: i32,
}

impl Iterator for Counter {
    type Item = i32;

    fn next(&mut self) -> Option<Self::Item> {
        self.count += 1;
        if self.count < 6 {
            Some(self.count)
        } else {
            None
        }
    }
```

```
}

fn main() {
    let counter = Counter { count: 0 };

    for number in counter {
        println!("{}", number);
    }
}
```

In this example, Counter is a custom data structure that implements the Iterator trait. Its next method increments the count and returns the next value until the count reaches 6.

Iterator Adapters: Enhancing Iterators for Functional Programming in Rust

Iterator adapters are powerful tools in Rust that allow you to transform and manipulate iterators in various ways. They provide a concise and expressive way to chain operations together, enabling you to perform complex data manipulations with ease. In this section, we'll explore some of the most common iterator adapters, including map, filter, fold, collect, and others, highlighting their functionality and how they can be used to write efficient and elegant functional code.

map: Transforming Elements

The map adapter applies a function to each element of an iterator, producing a new iterator with the transformed elements. This is particularly useful when you want to modify the values of an iterator without consuming it.

Example:

Rust

```rust
fn main() {
    let numbers = vec!;

    let squared_numbers: Vec<i32> = numbers
        .iter()
        .map(|x| x * x)
        .collect();

    println!("{:?}", squared_numbers); // Output:
}
```

In this example, map takes a closure |x| x * x that squares each element. The collect method then consumes the resulting iterator and gathers the squared numbers into a new vector.

filter: Selecting Elements

The filter adapter creates an iterator that yields only the elements of the original iterator that satisfy a given predicate function. This is useful for extracting specific elements from an iterator based on certain criteria.

Example:

```rust
fn main() {
    let numbers = vec!;

    let even_numbers: Vec<i32> = numbers
        .iter()
        .filter(|x| *x % 2 == 0)
        .collect();

    println!("{:?}", even_numbers); // Output:
}
```

In this example, filter takes a closure |x| *x % 2 == 0 that checks if a number is even. The collect method gathers the even numbers into a new vector.

fold: Accumulating Values

The fold adapter (also known as reduce) iterates over the elements of an iterator, accumulating a single result value. It takes an initial value and a closure that combines the current accumulator value with each element to produce a new accumulator value.

Example:

```
fn main() {
    let numbers = vec!;

    let sum: i32 = numbers
        .iter()
        .fold(0, |acc, x| acc + x);

    println!("{}", sum); // Output: 15
}
```

In this example, fold starts with an initial value of 0 and uses the closure |acc, x| acc + x to add each element to the accumulator, resulting in the sum of all elements.

collect: Gathering Elements

The collect adapter consumes an iterator and collects its elements into a collection, such as a vector, hash map, or string. This is often used as the final step in an iterator chain to gather the results of the transformations.

Example:

Rust

```
fn main() {
    let numbers = vec!;

    let doubled_numbers: Vec<i32> = numbers
        .iter()
```

```
    .map(|x| x * 2)
    .collect();

  println!("{:?}", doubled_numbers); // Output:
}
```

In this example, collect gathers the doubled numbers from the map adapter into a new vector.

Other Iterator Adapters

The Iterator trait provides many other useful adapters, including:

- zip: Combines two iterators into a single iterator of pairs.
- enumerate: Adds a counter to each element, creating an iterator of tuples (index, element).
- skip: Skips the first n elements of an iterator.
- take: Takes the first n elements of an iterator.
- chain: Chains two iterators together, creating a new iterator that yields the elements of the first iterator followed by the elements of the second.
- cycle: Creates an iterator that repeats the elements of the original iterator endlessly.

Chaining Adapters

One of the most powerful features of iterator adapters is the ability to chain them together to perform complex data manipulations in a concise and readable way.

Example:

Rust

```
fn main() {
    let numbers = vec!;

    let result: Vec<i32> = numbers
        .iter()
        .filter(|x| *x % 2 == 0) // Filter for even numbers
        .map(|x| x * 3) // Triple each even number
        .enumerate() // Add a counter to each element
        .collect();

    println!("{:?}", result); // Output: [(0, 6), (1, 12)]
}
```

In this example, we chain filter, map, and enumerate to first select even numbers, then triple them, and finally add a counter to each element.

EXPLORING MORE ITERATOR ADAPTERS: Examples & Code

In our previous discussion, we covered some fundamental iterator adapters like map, filter, and fold. Now, let's delve deeper into the world of iterator adapters, exploring more specialized adapters with plenty of examples and code to illustrate their usage. Remember, these adapters provide powerful tools for manipulating iterators, enabling you to perform complex data transformations in a concise and expressive manner.

zip: Combining Iterators

The zip adapter combines two iterators into a single iterator of pairs. This is useful when you need to process elements from two different iterators simultaneously.

Example:

Rust

```
fn main() {

    let names = vec!["Alice", "Bob", "Charlie"];

    let scores = vec!;


    let zipped: Vec<(&str, i32)> = names

        .iter()

        .zip(scores.iter())

        .collect();
```

```
    println!("{:?}", zipped); // Output: [("Alice", 10), ("Bob",
20), ("Charlie", 30)]

}
```

In this example, zip combines the names and scores iterators, creating an iterator that yields pairs of names and scores. The collect method gathers these pairs into a new vector.

enumerate: Adding a Counter

The enumerate adapter adds a counter to each element of an iterator, creating an iterator of tuples (index, element). This is useful when you need to track the index of each element while iterating.

Example:

Rust

```
fn main() {

    let numbers = vec!;


    let enumerated: Vec<(usize, i32)> = numbers

        .iter()

        .enumerate()
```

```rust
    .collect();
```

```rust
    println!("{:?}", enumerated); // Output: [(0, 10), (1, 20), (2, 30)]
```

```rust
}
```

In this example, enumerate adds a counter to each element of the numbers iterator, resulting in an iterator of tuples containing the index and the corresponding value.

skip and take: Slicing Iterators

The skip adapter skips the first n elements of an iterator, while the take adapter takes the first n elements. These adapters are useful for slicing iterators and extracting specific portions of the data.

Example:

Rust

```rust
fn main() {

    let numbers = vec!;


    let skipped: Vec<i32> = numbers

        .iter()
```

```
        .skip(2) // Skip the first 2 elements

        .collect();


    println!("{:?}", skipped); // Output:


    let taken: Vec<i32> = numbers

        .iter()

        .take(3) // Take the first 3 elements

        .collect();


    println!("{:?}", taken); // Output:

}
```

In this example, skip(2) skips the first two elements of the numbers iterator, while take(3) takes the first three elements.

chain: Concatenating Iterators

The chain adapter concatenates two iterators, creating a new iterator that yields the elements of the first iterator followed by the elements of the second iterator.

Example:

Rust

```rust
fn main() {
    let numbers1 = vec!;

    let numbers2 = vec!;


    let chained: Vec<i32> = numbers1
        .iter()
        .chain(numbers2.iter())
        .collect();


    println!("{:?}", chained); // Output:
}
```

In this example, chain concatenates the numbers1 and numbers2 iterators, creating a new iterator that yields all the numbers in sequence.

cycle: Repeating Elements

The cycle adapter creates an iterator that repeats the elements of the original iterator endlessly. This can be useful for generating repeating patterns or sequences.

Example:

Rust

```
fn main() {

    let numbers = vec!;


    let repeated: Vec<i32> = numbers

        .iter()

        .cycle()

        .take(10) // Take the first 10 elements of the infinite cycle

        .collect();


    println!("{:?}", repeated); // Output:

}
```

In this example, cycle creates an infinite iterator that repeats the elements of numbers. We then use take(10) to limit the output to the first 10 elements of this infinite sequence.

These examples showcase the versatility and power of iterator adapters in Rust. By combining and chaining these adapters, you can perform complex data manipulations with ease, writing concise and expressive code that is well-suited for functional programming paradigms. Remember, these adapters are lazy, meaning they only compute values when they are needed, which can improve performance by avoiding unnecessary computations.

Chaining Iterators for Complex Data Transformations in Rust

Chaining iterators is a powerful technique in Rust that allows you to perform complex data transformations in a concise and expressive manner. By combining multiple iterator adapters, you can create a pipeline of operations that sequentially transform the data, leading to elegant and efficient code. Let's explore the concept of chaining iterators in detail, understanding its benefits and how it can be applied to various scenarios.

The Power of Composability

Iterator adapters are designed to be composable, meaning you can chain them together to create complex data processing pipelines. Each adapter takes an iterator as input and produces a new iterator as output, allowing you to apply multiple transformations in sequence.

Example:

Rust

```
fn main() {
```

```
let numbers = vec!;


let result: Vec<i32> = numbers

    .iter()

    .filter(|x| *x % 2 == 0) // Filter for even numbers

    .map(|x| x * 3) // Triple each even number

    .collect();


    println!("{:?}", result); // Output:

}
```

In this example, we chain the filter and map adapters. The filter adapter selects only the even numbers from the numbers vector. The map adapter then triples each of these even numbers. Finally, the collect adapter gathers the resulting values into a new vector.

Benefits of Chaining Iterators

- Readability and Conciseness: Chaining iterators allows you to express complex data transformations in a clear and concise way, making your code easier to read and understand.

- Efficiency: Iterator adapters are lazy, meaning they only compute values when they are needed. This can improve performance by avoiding unnecessary computations.
- Flexibility: You can easily add or remove adapters in the chain to modify the data transformation pipeline, providing flexibility and adaptability.
- Reusability: You can reuse individual adapters or chains of adapters in different parts of your code, promoting code modularity and reducing duplication.

Practical Examples

Let's explore some practical examples of how chaining iterators can be used to solve real-world problems:

Example 1: Data Analysis

Imagine you have a dataset of student records, and you want to find the average score of students who passed a particular exam. You can achieve this by chaining iterators:

```rust
Rust

struct Student {

    name: String,

    score: i32,

}
```

```rust
fn main() {

    let students = vec![

        Student { name: "Alice".to_string(), score: 85 },

        Student { name: "Bob".to_string(), score: 60 },

        Student { name: "Charlie".to_string(), score: 90 },

    ];


    let average_passing_score: f64 = students

        .iter()

        .filter(|student| student.score >= 70) // Filter for passing students

        .map(|student| student.score as f64) // Convert scores to f64

        .sum::<f64>() / students.len() as f64; // Calculate the average


        println!("Average passing score: {}", average_passing_score);

}
```

In this example, we chain filter and map to first select passing students and then extract their scores as floating-point numbers. We then use sum to calculate the total score and divide it by the number of passing students to get the average.

Example 2: Text Processing

Let's say you have a string of text, and you want to extract all the words that start with a capital letter. You can achieve this by chaining iterators:

Rust

```
fn main() {

    let text = "This is an Example String with Some Capitalized Words.";


    let capitalized_words: Vec<&str> = text

        .split_whitespace() // Split the string into words

        .filter(|word| word.chars().next().unwrap().is_uppercase()) // Filter for capitalized words

        .collect();


    println!("{:?}", capitalized_words); // Output: ["This", "Example", "String", "Some", "Capitalized", "Words."]
```

```
}
```

In this example, we use split_whitespace to split the string into words. Then, we use filter to select words that start with a capital letter, and finally, we use collect to gather the capitalized words into a vector.

Example 3: Custom Data Structures

You can also chain iterators with custom data structures that implement the Iterator trait. This allows you to seamlessly integrate your custom data structures with Rust's iterator ecosystem.

Rust

```rust
struct Counter {

    count: i32,

}


impl Iterator for Counter {

    type Item = i32;


    fn next(&mut self) -> Option<Self::Item> {
```

```rust
        self.count += 1;

        if self.count < 6 {

            Some(self.count)

        } else {

            None

        }

    }

}


fn main() {

    let result: Vec<i32> = Counter { count: 0 }

        .filter(|x| x % 2 == 0) // Filter for even numbers

        .map(|x| x * 2) // Double each even number

        .collect();


    println!("{:?}", result); // Output:

}
```

In this example, we chain filter and map with a custom iterator Counter. The filter adapter selects even numbers generated by the Counter, and the map adapter doubles these even numbers.

These examples demonstrate the versatility and power of chaining iterators in Rust. By combining multiple adapters, you can create complex data transformation pipelines that are concise, readable, and efficient.

Practical Examples of Iterators in Rust: Processing Files and Performing Calculations

Iterators in Rust provide a powerful and efficient way to work with collections of data, enabling you to process elements sequentially without having to worry about the underlying implementation details. In this section, we'll explore some practical examples of how iterators can be used to process data from files and perform calculations on collections, showcasing their versatility and expressiveness in real-world scenarios.

Processing Data from Files

Reading and processing data from files is a common task in many applications. Iterators can simplify this process by providing a convenient way to iterate over the lines of a file.

Example: Calculating the Average from a File

Let's say you have a file named numbers.txt containing a list of numbers, one per line. You want to calculate the average of these numbers. You can achieve this using iterators as follows:

Rust

```rust
use std::fs::File;
use std::io::{BufRead, BufReader};

fn main() {
    let filename = "numbers.txt";
    let file = File::open(filename).expect("Failed to open file");
    let reader = BufReader::new(file);

    let mut sum = 0;
    let mut count = 0;

    for line in reader.lines() {
        let number: i32 = line
            .expect("Failed to read line")
            .parse()
            .expect("Failed to parse number");
        sum += number;
        count += 1;
    }

    let average = sum as f64 / count as f64;
    println!("Average: {}", average);
}
```

In this example, we open the file numbers.txt and create a BufReader to efficiently read the file line by line. The lines method on BufReader returns an iterator over the lines of the file.

We then use a for loop to iterate over the lines, parse each line as an integer, and update the sum and count. Finally, we calculate the average and print it to the console.

Example: Filtering Lines from a File

Imagine you have a log file containing various messages, and you want to extract only the error messages. You can achieve this using iterators and the filter adapter:

Rust

```rust
use std::fs::File;
use std::io::{BufRead, BufReader};

fn main() {
    let filename = "log.txt";
    let file = File::open(filename).expect("Failed to open file");
    let reader = BufReader::new(file);

    let error_messages: Vec<String> = reader
        .lines()
        .filter(|line| line.as_ref().unwrap().contains("error"))
        .collect();

    for message in error_messages {
        println!("{}", message);
```

```
    }
}
```

In this example, we use filter to select only the lines that contain the word "error". The collect adapter gathers these filtered lines into a vector of strings.

Performing Calculations on Collections

Iterators are also very useful for performing calculations on collections of data. The Iterator trait provides various adapters that simplify common calculations, such as sum, count, max, and min.

Example: Calculating the Sum of Squares

Let's say you have a vector of numbers, and you want to calculate the sum of their squares. You can achieve this using iterators and the map and sum adapters:

Rust

```
fn main() {
    let numbers = vec!;

    let sum_of_squares: i32 = numbers
        .iter()
        .map(|x| x * x)
        .sum();
```

```
    println!("Sum of squares: {}", sum_of_squares); // Output:
55
}
```

In this example, map squares each number in the vector, and sum adds up the squared values.

Example: Finding the Maximum and Minimum Values

You can use the max and min adapters to find the maximum and minimum values in a collection.

Rust

```
fn main() {
    let numbers = vec!;

    let max = numbers.iter().max().unwrap();
    let min = numbers.iter().min().unwrap();

    println!("Max: {}, Min: {}", max, min); // Output: Max: 9,
Min: 1
}
```

In this example, max and min find the maximum and minimum values in the numbers vector, respectively.

These examples demonstrate the versatility of iterators in Rust for processing data from files and performing calculations on collections. By leveraging the power of iterators and their adapters, you can write concise and efficient code that is well-suited for various data processing tasks, embracing the principles of functional programming.

CHAPTER 5

Closures: Capturing and Computing

Understanding Closures: Anonymous Functions with a Twist

Closures in Rust are a powerful tool that enhances the functional programming experience. They are essentially anonymous functions that can capture variables from their surrounding scope, allowing you to create flexible and reusable code blocks. Let's delve into the details of closures, understanding their syntax and how they work.

Defining Closures: Concise and Flexible

Closures are defined using a concise syntax that resembles lambda expressions in other languages. They are typically enclosed in vertical bars ‖, followed by an optional parameter list, an optional type annotation for the parameters, and a code block within curly braces {}.

```Rust
let add_one = |x| x + 1; // Closure that adds 1 to its input

let result = add_one(5);
```

```rust
println!("{}", result); // Output: 6
```

In this example, add_one is a closure that takes a single parameter x and returns x + 1. The type of x is inferred to be i32 based on its usage.

Type Inference: Less Boilerplate

One of the convenient features of closures is that their parameter and return types can often be inferred by the compiler. This reduces the amount of boilerplate code you need to write, making your code more concise and readable.

Rust

```rust
let square = |x| x * x; // Type inference for both parameter and return type
```

In this example, the compiler infers that square takes an i32 as input and returns an i32 as output.

Capturing Variables: Accessing the Surrounding Scope

Closures can capture variables from their surrounding scope, allowing them to access and manipulate data that is not explicitly passed as parameters. This is a key feature that distinguishes closures from regular functions.

Rust

```
fn main() {
    let factor = 3;
    let multiplier = |x| x * factor; // Closure capturing the factor
variable

    println!("{}", multiplier(5)); // Output: 15
}
```

In this example, the multiplier closure captures the factor variable from its surrounding scope. This allows the closure to use the value of factor even though it is not explicitly passed as a parameter.

Closure Traits: Fn, FnMut, and FnOnce

Closures in Rust implement one of three traits: Fn, FnMut, or FnOnce. These traits determine how the closure interacts with the captured variables.

- Fn: Represents a closure that borrows its captured variables immutably. This means the closure can read the captured variables but cannot modify them.
- FnMut: Represents a closure that mutably borrows its captured variables. This means the closure can modify the captured variables.
- FnOnce: Represents a closure that takes ownership of its captured variables. This means the closure can consume the captured variables, preventing them from being used again.

The compiler automatically determines which trait to implement for a closure based on how it uses the captured variables.

Closures and Higher-Order Functions: A Powerful Combination

Closures are often used in conjunction with higher-order functions, which are functions that take other functions as arguments or return functions as results. This combination enables powerful functional programming patterns.

Example:

Rust

```rust
fn map<F>(f: F, v: Vec<i32>) -> Vec<i32>
where
    F: Fn(i32) -> i32,
{
    let mut result = Vec::new();
    for x in v {
        result.push(f(x));
    }
    result
}

fn main() {
    let numbers = vec!;
    let doubled_numbers = map(|x| x * 2, numbers); // Passing a closure to map
    println!("{:?}", doubled_numbers); // Output:
```

```
}
```

In this example, map is a higher-order function that takes a closure f as an argument. The closure is applied to each element of the vector v, producing a new vector with the transformed elements.

Benefits of Closures

- Conciseness: Closures provide a concise syntax for defining anonymous functions, reducing boilerplate code.
- Flexibility: Closures can capture variables from their surrounding scope, allowing them to adapt to different contexts.
- Reusability: Closures can be passed as arguments to higher-order functions, promoting code reuse and modularity.
- Expressiveness: Closures enable powerful functional programming patterns, making your code more expressive and easier to understand.

By understanding closures and their syntax, you can unlock their full potential in your Rust programs. They are a valuable tool for writing concise, flexible, and reusable code, especially in the context of functional programming.

Closures and Capturing: Understanding Move Semantics

Closures in Rust have the ability to capture variables from their surrounding scope, allowing them to access and manipulate data that is not explicitly passed as parameters. This capturing behavior is governed by move semantics, which determine how ownership of the captured variables is transferred or shared between the closure and its environment. Let's explore move semantics in detail, understanding how they affect closure behavior and how to manage variable capturing effectively.

Move Semantics: Ownership Transfer

Move semantics in Rust dictate that when a value is assigned to a new variable or passed to a function, ownership of that value is transferred to the new owner. This prevents accidental sharing of mutable data and ensures memory safety.

```
Rust

let s1 = String::from("hello");
let s2 = s1; // Ownership of the string data is moved from s1 to
s2
// println!("{}", s1); // This would cause an error because s1 no
longer owns the string
```

In this example, ownership of the string data is moved from s1 to s2. This means s1 can no longer be used to access the string.

Capturing by Value: Taking Ownership

When a closure captures a variable by value, it takes ownership of that variable. This means the variable is moved into the closure, and its original binding becomes invalid.

Rust

```
fn main() {
    let x = 5;
    let capture_x = || x + 1; // Closure captures x by value
(taking ownership)

    // println!("{}", x); // This would cause an error because x
has been moved into the closure
    println!("{}", capture_x()); // Output: 6
}
```

In this example, the capture_x closure captures x by value, taking ownership of it. This means x is no longer accessible outside the closure.

Capturing by Reference: Borrowing

Closures can also capture variables by reference, either immutably or mutably. This allows the closure to access the variable without taking ownership, preserving the original binding.

Rust

```
fn main() {
    let x = 5;
```

```rust
    let print_x = || println!("{}", x); // Closure captures x by
immutable reference

    print_x(); // Output: 5
    println!("{}", x); // This is okay because x is still accessible
}
```

In this example, print_x captures x by immutable reference, allowing it to read the value of x without taking ownership.

Capturing by Mutable Reference: Modifying Variables

Closures can also capture variables by mutable reference, allowing them to modify the captured variable.

Rust

```rust
fn main() {
    let mut x = 5;
    let increment_x = || x += 1; // Closure captures x by mutable
reference

    increment_x();
    println!("{}", x); // Output: 6
}
```

In this example, increment_x captures x by mutable reference, allowing it to modify the value of x.

Choosing the Capture Method

The choice of how to capture a variable depends on how the closure intends to use it.

- If the closure needs to take ownership of the variable, capture it by value.
- If the closure only needs to read the variable, capture it by immutable reference.
- If the closure needs to modify the variable, capture it by mutable reference.

Implications for Functional Programming

Move semantics and capturing in closures have important implications for functional programming:

- Immutability: Capturing by value enforces immutability of the captured variable within the closure, aligning with functional programming principles.
- Data Ownership and Transformation: Closures can be used to create functions that transform data without modifying the original data, promoting immutability and safe data handling.
- Function Composition: Closures with captured variables can be used to create specialized functions that encapsulate specific behavior, facilitating function composition and code reuse.

Closures with Iterators and Higher-Order Functions: A Powerful Combination

Closures and iterators are a dynamic duo in Rust's functional programming toolkit. Combining closures with iterators and other higher-order functions unlocks a world of possibilities for concise, expressive, and efficient data manipulation. Let's explore how closures enhance the use of iterators and higher-order functions, enabling you to write elegant and functional code.

Closures as Iterator Adapters

Closures seamlessly integrate with iterator adapters, providing a flexible way to customize their behavior. Adapters like map, filter, and fold take closures as arguments, allowing you to define specific transformations or predicates on the fly.

Example: map with Closures

Rust

```
fn main() {
    let numbers = vec!;

    let doubled_numbers: Vec<i32> = numbers
        .iter()
        .map(|x| x * 2) // Closure that doubles each element
        .collect();

    println!("{:?}", doubled_numbers); // Output:
}
```

In this example, the map adapter takes a closure |x| x * 2 that doubles each element of the numbers iterator. This closure defines the transformation logic inline, making the code concise and readable.

Example: filter with Closures

Rust

```
fn main() {
    let numbers = vec!;

    let even_numbers: Vec<i32> = numbers
        .iter()
            .filter(|x| *x % 2 == 0) // Closure that filters for even
numbers
        .collect();

    println!("{:?}", even_numbers); // Output:
}
```

Here, the filter adapter takes a closure |x| *x % 2 == 0 that checks if a number is even. This closure acts as a predicate, determining which elements should be included in the filtered iterator.

Closures with fold for Custom Reductions

The fold adapter (also known as reduce) provides a powerful way to accumulate values from an iterator. Closures allow you to define custom accumulation logic, adapting the fold operation to various scenarios.

Example: Calculating the Product of Elements

Rust

```
fn main() {
    let numbers = vec!;

    let product: i32 = numbers
        .iter()
            .fold(1, |acc, x| acc * x); // Closure that multiplies the
accumulator by each element

    println!("{}", product); // Output: 120
}
```

In this example, the fold adapter starts with an initial value of 1 and uses the closure |acc, x| acc * x to multiply the accumulator by each element, resulting in the product of all elements.

Closures for Custom Sorting

Closures can be used with the sort_by_key and sort_by methods on vectors to define custom sorting logic.

Example: Sorting by String Length

```
fn main() {
    let mut words = vec!["apple", "banana", "cherry", "date"];

    words.sort_by_key(|word| word.len()); // Sorting by string
length

    println!("{:?}", words); // Output: ["date", "apple", "cherry",
"banana"]
}
```

In this example, sort_by_key takes a closure |word| word.len() that extracts the length of each word. The vector is then sorted based on these lengths.

Closures with Custom Iterators

Closures can also be used to define the behavior of custom iterators. By implementing the Iterator trait for your own data structures and using closures in the next method, you can create iterators with tailored functionality.

Example: Generating Fibonacci Numbers

```
struct Fibonacci {
    current: u64,
```

```rust
    next: u64,
}

impl Iterator for Fibonacci {
    type Item = u64;

    fn next(&mut self) -> Option<Self::Item> {
        let new_next = self.current + self.next;
        self.current = self.next;
        self.next = new_next;
        Some(self.current)
    }
}

fn main() {
    let fib = Fibonacci { current: 1, next: 1 };

    for number in fib.take(10) {
        println!("{}", number); // Output: 1, 1, 2, 3, 5, 8, 13, 21,
34, 55
    }
}
```

In this example, the Fibonacci struct implements the Iterator trait. Its next method uses a closure to calculate the next Fibonacci number in the sequence.

Benefits of Using Closures

- Conciseness: Closures provide a concise syntax for defining anonymous functions, reducing boilerplate code.
- Flexibility: Closures can capture variables from their surrounding scope, allowing them to adapt to different contexts.
- Expressiveness: Closures enable you to define custom behavior for iterators and higher-order functions, making your code more expressive and easier to understand.

Closure Traits: Fn, FnMut, and FnOnce - Understanding Closure Behavior

Closures in Rust are versatile tools for functional programming, but their behavior can vary depending on how they interact with the variables they capture from their surrounding scope. To manage this interaction, Rust provides three closure traits: Fn, FnMut, and FnOnce. These traits define the borrowing behavior of closures, determining whether they borrow captured variables immutably, mutably, or take ownership of them. Let's explore these traits in detail, understanding their implications and how they influence closure usage.

Fn: Immutable Borrowing

The Fn trait represents closures that borrow their captured variables immutably. This means the closure can read the captured variables but cannot modify them. Fn closures are suitable for situations where you need to access data from the surrounding scope without altering it.

Example:

Rust

```
fn main() {
    let message = "Hello, world!".to_string();
    let print_message = || println!("{}", message); // Closure captures message immutably

    print_message(); // Output: Hello, world!
    println!("{}", message); // message is still accessible because it was borrowed immutably
}
```

In this example, the print_message closure captures the message variable by immutable reference. This allows the closure to read the value of message without taking ownership or modifying it.

FnMut: Mutable Borrowing

The FnMut trait represents closures that mutably borrow their captured variables. This means the closure can modify the captured variables. FnMut closures are useful when you need to update data from the surrounding scope within the closure.

Example:

```
fn main() {
    let mut counter = 0;
    let increment_counter = || counter += 1; // Closure captures
counter mutably

    increment_counter();
    increment_counter();
    println!("{}", counter); // Output: 2
}
```

In this example, the increment_counter closure captures the counter variable by mutable reference. This allows the closure to modify the value of counter, incrementing it with each call.

FnOnce: Taking Ownership

The FnOnce trait represents closures that take ownership of their captured variables. This means the closure consumes the captured variables, preventing them from being used again. FnOnce closures are suitable for situations where you need to move data into the closure or modify it in a way that invalidates its original binding.

Example:

Rust

```
fn main() {
    let message = "Hello, world!".to_string();
```

```
let consume_message = || {
    println!("{}", message);
        // message is dropped here because the closure takes
ownership
    };


    consume_message();
    // println!("{}", message); // This would cause an error
because message has been moved into the closure
}
```

In this example, the consume_message closure captures the message variable by value, taking ownership of it. This means message is no longer accessible outside the closure.

Trait Relationships: A Hierarchy of Borrowing

The closure traits have a hierarchical relationship:

- FnOnce: All closures implement FnOnce, as they can be called at least once.
- FnMut: Closures that implement FnMut also implement FnOnce, as mutable borrowing subsumes one-time consumption.
- Fn: Closures that implement Fn also implement FnMut and FnOnce, as immutable borrowing is a more restrictive form of borrowing.

Compiler Inference: Determining the Appropriate Trait

The Rust compiler automatically infers the appropriate trait to This relieves you from having to explicitly specify the trait in most cases.

Implications for Functional Programming

The closure traits and their borrowing behavior have important implications for functional programming:

- Immutability: Fn closures promote immutability by ensuring that captured variables are not modified, aligning with functional programming principles.
- Data Ownership and Transformation: FnOnce closures allow you to move data into closures, enabling transformations that consume the original data.
- Flexibility: The closure traits provide flexibility in how closures interact with their environment, allowing you to choose the appropriate borrowing behavior based on the specific needs of your code.

By understanding the closure traits Fn, FnMut, and FnOnce, you can write more expressive and functional code in Rust. These traits provide a clear framework for managing the borrowing behavior of closures, enabling you to create flexible and reusable code blocks that adapt to different contexts.

Closures in Action: Implementing Custom Iterators, Event Handlers, and Callbacks

Closures in Rust are versatile tools that can be applied to various scenarios beyond just iterator adapters. Their ability to capture variables from their surrounding scope and their concise syntax make them ideal for implementing custom iterators, event handlers, and callbacks. Let's explore these use cases in detail, showcasing the power and flexibility of closures in action.

Implementing Custom Iterators

Closures can be used to define the behavior of custom iterators, allowing you to create iterators that generate sequences of values based on specific logic. By implementing the Iterator trait for your own data structures and using closures in the next method, you can create iterators with tailored functionality.

Example: Generating a Sequence of Squares

```rust
Rust

struct SquareGenerator {
    current: i32,
}

impl Iterator for SquareGenerator {
    type Item = i32;

    fn next(&mut self) -> Option<Self::Item> {
        let result = self.current * self.current;
        self.current += 1;
        Some(result)
```

```
    }
}

fn main() {
    let squares = SquareGenerator { current: 1 };

    for number in squares.take(5) {
        println!("{}", number); // Output: 1, 4, 9, 16, 25
    }
}
```

In this example, the SquareGenerator struct implements the Iterator trait. Its next method uses a closure to calculate the square of the current number and then increments the current number. This creates an iterator that generates a sequence of squares.

Event Handlers: Responding to Events

Closures are well-suited for implementing event handlers, which are functions or code blocks that are executed in response to specific events, such as user input, network activity, or timer expirations.

Example: Button Click Handler

Rust

```
// Assume a GUI library with a Button and an on_click method
let button = Button::new("Click me!");
```

```rust
button.on_click(|| {
    println!("Button clicked!");
    // Perform actions in response to the button click
});
```

In this example, the on_click method takes a closure as an argument. This closure represents the event handler that will be executed when the button is clicked. The closure can capture variables from its surrounding scope, allowing it to access and modify data related to the button or the application state.

Callbacks: Asynchronous Operations

Closures can also be used as callbacks for asynchronous operations. Callbacks are functions that are executed after an asynchronous operation has completed, such as a network request or a file read.

Example: File Read Callback

Rust

```rust
// Assume a file I/O library with an async_read_file function
async_read_file("data.txt", |result| {
    match result {
        Ok(contents) => {
            println!("File contents: {}", contents);
            // Process the file contents
        }
```

```
    Err(error) => {
        println!("Error reading file: {}", error);
        // Handle the error
    }
  }
});
```

In this example, async_read_file takes a filename and a closure as arguments. The closure represents the callback function that will be executed once the file reading operation is complete. The closure receives the result of the operation, which can be either successful (Ok) or an error (Err).

Benefits of Using Closures

- Conciseness: Closures provide a concise syntax for defining anonymous functions, reducing boilerplate code.
- Flexibility: Closures can capture variables from their surrounding scope, allowing them to adapt to different contexts.
- Readability: Using closures for event handlers and callbacks can improve code readability by keeping the event handling logic close to where the event is triggered.
- Code Organization: Closures can help organize code by encapsulating specific behavior related to events or asynchronous operations.

By leveraging closures for implementing custom iterators, event handlers, and callbacks, you can write more expressive, flexible, and organized code in Rust. Closures provide a powerful tool for adapting to various scenarios, enhancing your ability to write elegant and efficient functional programs.

CHAPTER 6

Working with Options and Results: Handling Uncertainty

The Option Type: Embracing the Absence of Values

In the realm of programming, it's not uncommon to encounter situations where a value might be present or absent. Traditional approaches often rely on special values like null or -1 to represent missing data, but these can lead to errors and unexpected behavior if not handled carefully. Rust takes a more robust approach with the Option type, a core enum that provides a safe and expressive way to handle the possibility of a missing value. Let's explore the Option type in detail, understanding its significance and how it enhances the safety and clarity of your Rust code.

Understanding the Option Enum

The Option type is an enum that represents the presence or absence of a value. It has two variants:

- Some(T): Represents the presence of a value of type T.
- None: Represents the absence of a value.

This simple yet powerful structure allows you to explicitly express the possibility of a missing value, making your code more robust and predictable.

Why Use Option?

The Option type offers several advantages over traditional approaches for handling missing values:

- Explicitness: The Option type forces you to explicitly handle the possibility of a missing value, preventing unexpected errors that can occur when assuming a value is always present.
- Safety: The compiler ensures that you handle both the Some and None cases when working with Option values, preventing runtime errors due to unhandled null or undefined values.
- Clarity: The Option type makes your code more readable and easier to understand by clearly indicating where a value might be missing.

Using Option in Practice

Let's explore some common ways to use the Option type in your Rust code:

- Returning a Potentially Missing Value: When a function might return a value or indicate that the value is not found, you can use Option as the return type.

```rust
fn find_user(username: &str) -> Option<User> {
    // ... logic to search for the user ...
    if let Some(user) = users.get(username) {
        Some(*user)
    } else {
        None
    }
}
```

In this example, find_user returns an Option<User>. If the user is found, it returns Some(user); otherwise, it returns None.

- Handling Missing Values: When working with Option values, you need to handle both the Some and None cases. Pattern matching provides an elegant way to do this.

Rust

```
let user = find_user("johndoe");

match user {
    Some(user) => println!("User found: {}", user.username),
    None => println!("User not found"),
}
```

In this example, we use match to handle the different cases of the Option value returned by find_user.

- Extracting Values: You can extract the value from a Some variant using various methods, such as unwrap (which panics if the value is None), expect (which allows you to provide a custom error message), or pattern matching.

Rust

```
let user = find_user("johndoe").expect("User not found"); //
Extract the value or panic with a message

if let Some(user) = find_user("janedoe") {
    // ... use the user value ...
```

}

- Default Values: You can provide a default value if the Option is None using the unwrap_or method.

Rust

```
let score = some_option.unwrap_or(0); // Use 0 as the default value if some_option is None
```

- Chaining Operations: The Option type provides various methods for chaining operations, such as map, and_then, and or_else, allowing you to perform transformations and handle different cases in a functional style.

```
let result = find_user("johndoe")
    .map(|user| user.email) // Extract the email if the user is
found
    .and_then(|email| send_email(email)); // Send an email if the
email is present
```

THE *Option* TYPE IN RUST: *A Deep Dive with Examples*

In previous discussions, we introduced the Option type as a powerful tool for handling the possibility of missing values in Rust. Now, let's solidify your understanding with more examples and code snippets, demonstrating how to effectively use Option in various scenarios.

Example 1: Returning a Potentially Missing Value

Let's say you have a function that searches for a user in a database. The user might exist or not. Using Option, you can express this possibility explicitly:

Rust

```rust
struct User {

    username: String,

    email: String,

}

fn find_user(username: &str, users: &Vec<User>) ->
Option<User> {

    for user in users {

        if user.username == username {

            return Some(user.clone()); // Found the user

        }

    }

    None // User not found

}

fn main() {

    let users = vec![
```

```rust
        User { username: "Alice".to_string(), email:
"alice@example.com".to_string() },

        User { username: "Bob".to_string(), email:
"bob@example.com".to_string() },

    ];

    let user = find_user("Alice", &users);

    println!("{:?}", user); // Output: Some(User { username:
"Alice", email: "alice@example.com" })

    let user = find_user("Charlie", &users);

    println!("{:?}", user); // Output: None

}
```

In this example, find_user returns Some(user) if the user is found, and None if not. This clearly communicates the possibility of a missing value.

Example 2: Handling Option Values with match

When working with Option values, you need to handle both the Some and None cases. The match expression provides an elegant way to do this:

Rust

```rust
fn main() {

    let some_number = Some(5);

    let no_number: Option<i32> = None;

    match some_number {

        Some(number) => println!("The number is {}", number),

        None => println!("No number provided"),

    }

    match no_number {

        Some(number) => println!("The number is {}", number),

        None => println!("No number provided"),

    }

}
```

This code demonstrates how match handles both cases of an Option.

Example 3: Extracting Values Safely

You can extract the value from a Some variant using various methods:

- unwrap(): Returns the value if Some, panics if None.
- expect(): Similar to unwrap, but allows you to provide a custom panic message.
- Pattern matching: Safe and expressive way to extract the value.

Rust

```rust
fn main() {

    let some_number = Some(5);

    let number = some_number.unwrap(); // Safe to unwrap
because we know it's Some

    println!("{}", number); // Output: 5

    let no_number: Option<i32> = None;

    // let number = no_number.unwrap(); // This would panic!
```

```rust
    if let Some(number) = no_number {

        println!("{}", number);

    } else {

        println!("No number provided");

    }

}
```

This example demonstrates safe value extraction using pattern matching and unwrap().

Example 4: Providing Default Values

The unwrap_or method provides a default value if the Option is None:

Rust

```rust
fn main() {

    let some_number = Some(5);

    let no_number: Option<i32> = None;
```

```
let number1 = some_number.unwrap_or(0);

println!("{}", number1); // Output: 5

let number2 = no_number.unwrap_or(0);

println!("{}", number2); // Output: 0

}
```

This shows how unwrap_or provides a fallback value when the Option is None.

Example 5: Chaining Operations

Option provides methods for chaining operations, like map, and_then, and or_else:

Rust

```
fn main() {

    let some_number = Some(5);

    let result = some_number

        .map(|x| x * 2) // Double the value if Some
```

```
    .and_then(|x| if x > 10 { Some(x) } else { None }) // Filter
for values greater than 10

        .or_else(|| Some(10)); // Provide a default value of 10 if
None

    println!("{:?}", result); // Output: Some(10)


}
```

This demonstrates how to chain operations on Option values for more complex logic.

Option and Functional Programming

The Option type aligns well with functional programming principles:

- Explicitness: It forces you to explicitly handle the possibility of missing values, promoting code clarity and preventing errors.
- Immutability: The Option type is immutable, encouraging you to treat data as immutable values and perform transformations without side effects.
- Composability: The Option type provides methods for chaining operations, enabling you to compose complex logic from simpler functions.

By understanding and utilizing the Option type, you can write more robust, predictable, and functional code in Rust. It provides a safe and expressive way to handle the possibility of missing values, enhancing the clarity and maintainability of your programs.

The Result Type: Error Handling, the Functional Way

In the world of programming, errors are inevitable. Whether it's a failed network request, an invalid user input, or a missing file, things can go wrong, and your code needs to be prepared to handle these situations gracefully. In Rust, the Result type provides a powerful and expressive mechanism for handling potential errors in a functional and safe manner. Let's delve into the details of the Result type, understanding its significance and how it enhances the robustness and reliability of your Rust code.

Understanding the Result Enum

The Result type is an enum that represents the outcome of an operation that can either succeed or fail. It has two variants:

- Ok(T): Represents a successful operation, carrying a value of type T.
- Err(E): Represents a failed operation, carrying an error value of type E.

This structure allows you to explicitly express the possibility of an error and handle both success and failure cases in a structured way.

Why Use Result?

The Result type offers several advantages over traditional error-handling approaches like exceptions or error codes:

- Explicitness: The Result type forces you to explicitly handle the possibility of an error, preventing unexpected crashes or undefined behavior that can occur when errors are not properly addressed.
- Safety: The compiler ensures that you handle both the Ok and Err cases when working with Result values, preventing runtime errors due to unhandled exceptions or ignored error codes.
- Clarity: The Result type makes your code more readable and easier to understand by clearly indicating where errors might occur and how they are handled.
- Composability: The Result type provides methods for chaining operations and combining results, enabling you to handle errors in a functional and composable manner.

Using Result in Practice

Let's explore some common ways to use the Result type in your Rust code:

- Returning Potentially Failing Operations: When a function might succeed or fail, you can use Result as the return type.

Rust

```
fn read_file(filename: &str) -> Result<String, std::io::Error> {
    // ... logic to read the file ...
    let contents = std::fs::read_to_string(filename)?; // Propagate any errors using the ? operator
    Ok(contents)
}
```

In this example, read_file returns a Result<String, std::io::Error>. If the file is read successfully, it returns Ok(contents); otherwise, it returns an Err with the corresponding std::io::Error.

- Handling Errors: When working with Result values, you need to handle both the Ok and Err cases. Pattern matching provides an elegant way to do this.

Rust

```
let result = read_file("data.txt");

match result {
    Ok(contents) => println!("File contents: {}", contents),
    Err(error) => println!("Error reading file: {}", error),
}
```

In this example, we use match to handle the different cases of the Result value returned by read_file.

- Propagating Errors: The ? operator provides a concise way to propagate errors up the call stack. If an error occurs, the ? operator will return the error from the current function.

Rust

```
fn process_data(filename: &str) -> Result<(), std::io::Error> {
    let contents = read_file(filename)?; // Propagate any errors from read_file
```

```
    // ... process the data ...
    Ok(())
}
```

In this example, the ? operator after read_file(filename) will propagate any errors returned by read_file up to the caller of process_data.

- Chaining Operations: The Result type provides methods for chaining operations, such as map, and_then, and or_else, allowing you to perform transformations and handle different cases in a functional style.

Rust

```
let result = read_file("data.txt")
    .map(|contents| contents.to_uppercase()) // Convert the contents to uppercase if successful
    .and_then(|uppercase_contents| write_file("output.txt", uppercase_contents)); // Write the uppercase contents to a new file
```

Result and Functional Programming

The Result type aligns well with functional programming principles:

- Explicitness: It forces you to explicitly handle the possibility of errors, promoting code clarity and preventing unexpected behavior.
- Immutability: The Result type is immutable, encouraging you to treat data as immutable values and perform transformations without side effects.
- Composability: The Result type provides methods for chaining operations, enabling you to compose complex logic from simpler functions.

By understanding and utilizing the Result type, you can write more robust, reliable, and functional code in Rust. It provides a safe and expressive way to handle potential errors, enhancing the clarity and maintainability of your programs.

Pattern Matching and Combinators: Elegant Error Handling and Control Flow with Option and Result

In Rust, Option and Result are powerful enums that provide safe and expressive ways to handle missing values and potential errors, respectively. Pattern matching and combinators offer elegant mechanisms for working with these enums, enabling you to write concise and readable code while maintaining safety and control flow. Let's explore these concepts in detail, understanding how they enhance your ability to handle various scenarios in a functional and idiomatic manner.

Pattern Matching: Deconstructing Enums

Pattern matching is a fundamental construct in Rust that allows you to compare a value against a series of patterns and execute different code blocks based on which pattern matches. It's particularly well-suited for working with enums like Option and Result, as it allows you to deconstruct the enum and access its inner values or handle different cases based on its variants.

Example: Matching on Option

Rust

```
fn main() {
    let some_number = Some(5);
    let no_number: Option<i32> = None;

    match some_number {
        Some(number) => println!("The number is: {}", number),
        None => println!("No number provided."),
    }

    match no_number {
        Some(number) => println!("The number is: {}", number),
```

```
      None => println!("No number provided."),
   }
}
```

In this example, match deconstructs the Option values, binding the inner value to number if the variant is Some and executing the corresponding code block.

Example: Matching on Result

Rust

```
fn divide(x: i32, y: i32) -> Result<i32, String> {
   if y == 0 {
      Err("Division by zero".to_string())
   } else {
      Ok(x / y)
   }
}

fn main() {
   let result = divide(10, 2);

   match result {
      Ok(value) => println!("Result: {}", value),
      Err(message) => println!("Error: {}", message),
   }
}
```

Here, match handles both the Ok and Err variants of the Result returned by divide, allowing you to perform different actions based on the outcome of the operation.

Combinators: Chaining and Composing Operations

Combinators are methods provided by Option and Result that enable you to chain operations and handle different cases in a functional and expressive way. They provide alternatives to explicit pattern matching, often leading to more concise and readable code.

Example: map for Option

Rust

```
fn main() {
    let some_number = Some(5);

    let doubled_number = some_number.map(|x| x * 2);
    println!("{:?}", doubled_number); // Output: Some(10)
}
```

The map combinator applies a function to the value inside Some and returns a new Option with the transformed value. If the original Option is None, map returns None directly.

Example: and_then for Result

Rust

```
fn sqrt(x: i32) -> Result<f64, String> {
    if x < 0 {
            Err("Cannot calculate square root of a negative number".to_string())
    } else {
        Ok((x as f64).sqrt())
    }
}

fn main() {
    let result = divide(10, 2).and_then(sqrt); // Chain divide and sqrt operations

    match result {
        Ok(value) => println!("Square root of result: {}", value),
        Err(message) => println!("Error: {}", message),
    }
}
```

The and_then combinator allows you to chain operations that return Result. If the first operation is Ok, and_then applies the provided function to the Ok value. If the first operation is Err, and_then returns the Err directly.

Example: unwrap_or for Option

Rust

```
fn main() {
    let some_number = Some(5);
    let no_number: Option<i32> = None;

    let number1 = some_number.unwrap_or(0);
    println!("{}", number1); // Output: 5

    let number2 = no_number.unwrap_or(0);
    println!("{}", number2); // Output: 0
}
```

The unwrap_or combinator provides a default value if the Option is None.

Other Combinators:

Option and Result offer a variety of other combinators, including:

- map_err: Applies a function to the error value inside Err.
- or_else: Provides an alternative Option or Result if the original is None or Err.
- unwrap_or_else: Similar to unwrap_or, but allows you to provide a closure to generate the default value.

EXPLORING COMBINATORS FOR *Option* AND *Result:* Examples and Code

In our previous discussions, we introduced pattern matching as a way to handle different cases within Option and Result. Now, let's dive deeper into the world of combinators, exploring various methods that provide elegant alternatives to pattern matching for manipulating and chaining operations on these powerful enums. Remember that combinators can lead to more concise and readable code while maintaining safety and control flow.

map: Transforming Values

The map combinator applies a function to the value inside Some or Ok, returning a new Option or Result with the transformed value. If the original value is None or Err, map returns None or Err directly.

Example with Option:

Rust

```rust
fn main() {

    let some_number = Some(5);

    let doubled_number = some_number.map(|x| x * 2);

    println!("{:?}", doubled_number); // Output: Some(10)

    let no_number: Option<i32> = None;
```

```rust
    let doubled_no_number = no_number.map(|x| x * 2);

    println!("{:?}", doubled_no_number); // Output: None

}
```

Example with Result:

Rust

```rust
fn stringify(x: i32) -> String {

    x.to_string()

}

fn main() {

    let result: Result<i32, String> = Ok(5);

    let stringified_result = result.map(stringify);

    println!("{:?}", stringified_result); // Output: Ok("5")

    let error_result: Result<i32, String> = Err("Error!".to_string());
```

```rust
let stringified_error_result = error_result.map(stringify);

    println!("{:?}", stringified_error_result);  // Output:
Err("Error!")


}
```

map_err: Transforming Errors

The map_err combinator is similar to map, but it applies a function to the error value inside Err, returning a new Result with the transformed error. If the original value is Ok, map_err returns Ok directly.

Example:

Rust

```rust
fn main() {

    let result: Result<i32, String> = Err("Error!".to_string());

        let mapped_error_result = result.map_err(|err|
err.to_uppercase());

        println!("{:?}", mapped_error_result);  // Output:
Err("ERROR!")
```

```
}
```

and_then: Chaining Operations

The and_then combinator allows you to chain operations that return Option or Result. If the first operation is Some or Ok, and_then applies the provided function to the value inside. If the first operation is None or Err, and_then returns None or Err directly.

Example with Option:

Rust

```
fn sqrt(x: i32) -> Option<f64> {

    if x >= 0 {

        Some((x as f64).sqrt())

    } else {

        None

    }

}
```

```rust
fn main() {

    let some_number = Some(9);

    let result = some_number.and_then(sqrt);

    println!("{:?}", result); // Output: Some(3.0)

    let negative_number = Some(-9);

    let result = negative_number.and_then(sqrt);

    println!("{:?}", result); // Output: None

}
```

Example with Result:

Rust

```rust
fn divide(x: i32, y: i32) -> Result<i32, String> {

    if y == 0 {

        Err("Division by zero".to_string())
```

```rust
    } else {

        Ok(x / y)

    }

}

fn main() {

    let result = divide(10, 2).and_then(sqrt);

    println!("{:?}", result); // Output: Ok(2.236068)

    let result = divide(10, 0).and_then(sqrt);

    println!("{:?}", result); // Output: Err("Division by zero")

}
```

or_else: Providing Alternatives

The or_else combinator provides an alternative Option or
Result if the original value is None or Err.

Example with Option:

Rust

```
fn main() {

    let no_number: Option<i32> = None;

    let alternative = no_number.or_else(|| Some(10));

    println!("{:?}", alternative); // Output: Some(10)

}
```

Example with Result:

Rust

```
fn main() {

    let result: Result<i32, String> = Err("Error!".to_string());

    let alternative = result.or_else(|_| Ok(10));

    println!("{:?}", alternative); // Output: Ok(10)

}
```

unwrap_or_else: Generating Default Values

The unwrap_or_else combinator is similar to unwrap_or, but it allows you to provide a closure to generate the default value.

Example:

Rust

```rust
fn main() {

    let no_number: Option<i32> = None;

    let number = no_number.unwrap_or_else(|| {

        println!("Generating default value...");

        10

    });

    println!("{}", number); // Output: Generating default value...
10

}
```

Benefits of Pattern Matching and Combinators

- Conciseness: Pattern matching and combinators provide concise ways to handle different cases and chain operations, reducing boilerplate code.
- Readability: They make your code more readable and easier to understand by clearly expressing the intent of your error handling and control flow logic.
- Safety: Pattern matching ensures that you handle all possible cases, while combinators provide safe ways to chain operations and propagate errors.
- Functional Style: They promote a functional programming style by encouraging immutability and composability.

These examples demonstrate the versatility and power of combinators for working with Option and Result in Rust. By using combinators, you can write concise, readable, and functional code that handles missing values and potential errors in an elegant and idiomatic manner.

Error Handling in a Functional Style: Embracing Result and Combinators

In Rust, error handling takes a functional and expressive approach, primarily through the Result type and its associated combinators. This approach aligns well with the principles of functional programming, promoting immutability, composability, and explicit error handling. Let's explore error handling in a functional style, understanding how it enhances the robustness and clarity of your Rust code.

The Result Type: Representing Success or Failure

The Result type is an enum that represents the outcome of an operation that can either succeed or fail. It has two variants:

- Ok(T): Represents a successful operation, carrying a value of type T.
- Err(E): Represents a failed operation, carrying an error value of type E.

This structure allows you to explicitly express the possibility of an error and handle both success and failure cases in a structured way.

Functional Error Handling Principles

Functional error handling emphasizes the following principles:

- Explicitness: Errors are explicitly represented and handled, rather than being implicitly thrown as exceptions.
- Immutability: The Result type is immutable, encouraging you to treat errors as values and perform transformations without side effects.
- Composability: The Result type provides combinators for chaining operations and combining results, enabling you to handle errors in a functional and composable manner.

Combinators: Chaining and Composing Error Handling

Combinators are methods provided by the Result type that allow you to chain operations and handle different cases in a functional and expressive way. They provide alternatives to explicit pattern matching, often leading to more concise and readable code.

Example: map for Transforming Successful Results

Rust

```rust
fn stringify(x: i32) -> String {
    x.to_string()
}

fn main() {
    let result: Result<i32, String> = Ok(5);
    let stringified_result = result.map(stringify);
    println!("{:?}", stringified_result); // Output: Ok("5")
}
```

The map combinator applies a function to the value inside Ok and returns a new Result with the transformed value. If the original Result is Err, map returns Err directly.

Example: map_err for Transforming Errors

Rust

```
fn main() {
    let result: Result<i32, String> = Err("Error!".to_string());

    let mapped_error_result = result.map_err(|err| err.to_uppercase());
    println!("{:?}", mapped_error_result); // Output: Err("ERROR!")
}
```

The map_err combinator is similar to map, but it applies a function to the error value inside Err, returning a new Result with the transformed error. If the original Result is Ok, map_err returns Ok directly.

Example: and_then for Chaining Fallible Operations

Rust

```
fn sqrt(x: i32) -> Result<f64, String> {
    if x < 0 {
        Err("Cannot calculate square root of a negative number".to_string())
    } else {
        Ok((x as f64).sqrt())
    }
}
```

```
fn main() {
    let result = divide(10, 2).and_then(sqrt); // Chain divide and
sqrt operations

    match result {
        Ok(value) => println!("Square root of result: {}", value),
        Err(message) => println!("Error: {}", message),
    }
}
```

The and_then combinator allows you to chain operations that
return Result. If the first operation is Ok, and_then applies the
provided function to the Ok value. If the first operation is Err,
and_then returns the Err directly.

Example: or_else for Providing Alternative Results

Rust

```
fn main() {
    let result: Result<i32, String> = Err("Error!".to_string());
    let alternative = result.or_else(|_| Ok(10));
    println!("{:?}", alternative); // Output: Ok(10)
}
```

The or_else combinator provides an alternative Result if the original value is Err.

Example: unwrap_or_else for Generating Default Values

Rust

```rust
fn main() {
    let result: Result<i32, String> = Err("Error!".to_string());
    let number = result.unwrap_or_else(|_| {
        println!("Generating default value...");
        10
    });
    println!("{}", number); // Output: Generating default value...
10
}
```

The unwrap_or_else combinator is similar to unwrap_or, but it allows you to provide a closure to generate the default value.

Benefits of Functional Error Handling

- Explicitness: Errors are explicitly represented and handled, promoting code clarity and preventing unexpected behavior.

- Immutability: The Result type is immutable, encouraging you to treat errors as values and perform transformations without side effects.
- Composability: The Result type provides combinators for chaining operations and combining results, enabling you to handle errors in a functional and composable manner.
- Readability: Combinators can make your code more readable and easier to understand by clearly expressing the intent of your error handling logic.
- Safety: Combinators provide safe ways to chain operations and propagate errors, preventing runtime errors due to unhandled exceptions or ignored error codes.

By embracing functional error handling techniques, you can write more robust, reliable, and maintainable code in Rust. The Result type and its combinators provide a powerful and expressive way to handle errors, aligning with the principles of functional programming and enhancing the clarity and safety of your programs.

Practical Examples of Error Handling in Rust: Parsing, Reading Files, and Making Network Requests

Error handling is a crucial aspect of robust and reliable software development. In Rust, the Result type and its associated combinators provide a powerful and expressive way to handle errors in a functional and safe manner. Let's explore some practical examples of how error handling can be applied to common scenarios like parsing data, reading from files, and making network requests.

Parsing Data

Parsing data often involves handling potential errors due to invalid input formats or unexpected data values. The Result type allows you to gracefully handle these errors and provide informative feedback to the user.

Example: Parsing an Integer from a String

Rust

```
fn parse_integer(input: &str) -> Result<i32,
std::num::ParseIntError> {
   input.parse::<i32>()
}

fn main() {
   let result = parse_integer("123");
   match result {
      Ok(number) => println!("Parsed number: {}", number),
      Err(error) => println!("Error parsing number: {}", error),
   }

   let result = parse_integer("abc");
   match result {
      Ok(number) => println!("Parsed number: {}", number),
      Err(error) => println!("Error parsing number: {}", error),
   }
}
```

In this example, the parse_integer function attempts to parse an integer from a string. If the parsing is successful, it returns Ok(number); otherwise, it returns an Err with the corresponding ParseIntError. The match expression handles both cases, providing appropriate feedback to the user.

Reading from Files

Reading from files can also lead to errors due to file not found, permission issues, or corrupted data. The Result type allows you to handle these errors gracefully and prevent your program from crashing.

Example: Reading a File and Handling Errors

Rust

```
use std::fs::File;
use std::io::Read;

fn read_file_contents(filename: &str) -> Result<String, std::io::Error> {
    let mut file = File::open(filename)?;
    let mut contents = String::new();
    file.read_to_string(&mut contents)?;
    Ok(contents)
}
```

```rust
fn main() {
    let result = read_file_contents("data.txt");

    match result {
        Ok(contents) => println!("File contents: {}", contents),
        Err(error) => println!("Error reading file: {}", error),
    }
}
```

In this example, the read_file_contents function attempts to open a file and read its contents. If the operation is successful, it returns Ok(contents); otherwise, it returns an Err with the corresponding std::io::Error. The match expression handles both cases, providing appropriate feedback to the user.

Making Network Requests

Network requests are inherently prone to errors due to network connectivity issues, server errors, or timeouts. The Result type allows you to handle these errors gracefully and provide appropriate feedback to the user.

Example: Making a Network Request and Handling Errors

Rust

```rust
use reqwest;

async fn fetch_data(url: &str) -> Result<String,
reqwest::Error> {
    let response = reqwest::get(url).await?;
    let body = response.text().await?;
    Ok(body)
}

#[tokio::main]
async fn main() {
    let result = fetch_data("https://example.com/data");

    match result {
        Ok(data) => println!("Fetched data: {}", data),
        Err(error) => println!("Error fetching data: {}", error),
    }
}
```

In this example, the fetch_data function uses the reqwest crate to make a network request to the specified URL. If the request is successful, it returns Ok(body); otherwise, it returns an Err with the corresponding reqwest::Error. The match expression handles both cases, providing appropriate feedback to the user.

Benefits of Functional Error Handling

- Explicitness: Errors are explicitly represented and handled, promoting code clarity and preventing unexpected behavior.
- Immutability: The Result type is immutable, encouraging you to treat errors as values and perform transformations without side effects.
- Composability: The Result type provides combinators for chaining operations and combining results, enabling you to handle errors in a functional and composable manner.
- Readability: The Result type and its combinators make your code more readable and easier to understand by clearly indicating where errors might occur and how they are handled.
- Safety: The compiler ensures that you handle both the Ok and Err cases when working with Result values, preventing runtime errors due to unhandled exceptions or ignored error codes.

By embracing functional error handling techniques, you can write more robust, reliable, and maintainable code in Rust. The Result type and its combinators provide a powerful and expressive way to handle errors, aligning with the principles of functional programming and enhancing the clarity and safety of your programs.

CHAPTER 7

Functional Design Patterns in Rust

Functional Design Patterns in Rust: Currying, Composition, and Memoization

Functional programming encourages the use of design patterns that promote code reusability, modularity, and elegance. In Rust, you can implement common functional design patterns like currying, composition, and memoization to enhance the structure and efficiency of your programs. Let's explore these patterns in detail, understanding their benefits and how they can be applied in various scenarios.

Currying: Transforming Functions

Currying is a technique that transforms a function that takes multiple arguments into a sequence of functions that each take a single argument. This allows you to partially apply a function by fixing some of its arguments, creating a new function with fewer arguments.

Example:

Rust

```rust
fn add(x: i32, y: i32) -> i32 {
    x + y
}

fn curried_add(x: i32) -> impl Fn(i32) -> i32 {
    move |y| add(x, y)
}

fn main() {
    let add_five = curried_add(5);
    println!("{}", add_five(3)); // Output: 8
}
```

In this example, curried_add takes one argument x and returns a closure that takes another argument y and adds it to x. This allows you to create specialized functions like add_five that add 5 to their input.

Benefits of Currying:

- Code Reusability: Currying allows you to create reusable functions that can be adapted to different contexts by partially applying arguments.
- Flexibility: It provides flexibility in how you apply arguments to a function, enabling you to fix some arguments while leaving others open for later.

- Improved Code Readability: Currying can make your code more readable by breaking down complex functions into smaller, more manageable units.

Function Composition: Combining Functions

Function composition is the process of combining multiple functions to create new functions. This allows you to build complex logic from simpler, reusable components.

Example:

Rust

```rust
fn double(x: i32) -> i32 {
    x * 2
}

fn square(x: i32) -> i32 {
    x * x
}

fn compose<A, B, C, F, G>(f: F, g: G) -> impl Fn(A) -> C
where
    F: Fn(B) -> C,
    G: Fn(A) -> B,
{
    move |x| f(g(x))
}

fn main() {
```

```
let double_then_square = compose(square, double);
println!("{}", double_then_square(3)); // Output: 36
}
```

In this example, compose takes two functions f and g and returns a new function that applies g to its input and then applies f to the result. This allows you to create functions like double_then_square that combine the effects of double and square.

Benefits of Function Composition:

- Modularity: Function composition promotes modularity by breaking down complex logic into smaller, reusable functions.
- Code Reusability: It allows you to reuse existing functions in new ways by combining them with other functions.
- Improved Code Readability: Function composition can make your code more readable by expressing complex operations as a sequence of simpler operations.

Memoization: Caching Results

Memoization is a technique that caches the results of expensive function calls, so that if the function is called again with the same arguments, the cached result is returned instead of recomputing it. This can significantly improve performance for functions with computationally intensive operations.

Example:

Rust

```rust
use std::collections::HashMap;

fn fibonacci(n: u64, cache: &mut HashMap<u64, u64>) -> u64 {
    if let Some(&result) = cache.get(&n) {
        return result;
    }

    let result = if n <= 1 {
        n
    } else {
        fibonacci(n - 1, cache) + fibonacci(n - 2, cache)
    };

    cache.insert(n, result);
    result
}

fn main() {
    let mut cache = HashMap::new();
    println!("{}", fibonacci(10, &mut cache)); // Output: 55
}
```

In this example, fibonacci calculates the nth Fibonacci number. The cache HashMap stores previously computed results. If the result for n is already in the cache, it is returned directly. Otherwise, the result is computed, stored in the cache, and then returned.

Benefits of Memoization:

- Performance Improvement: Memoization can significantly improve performance for functions with expensive computations by avoiding redundant calculations.
- Code Optimization: It can optimize code by reducing the number of times a computationally intensive function is executed.

FUNCTIONAL DESIGN PATTERNS IN RUST: A Deep Dive with Examples

In our previous discussion, we explored the concepts of currying, function composition, and memoization as powerful functional design patterns. Now, let's solidify your understanding with more examples and code snippets, demonstrating how to effectively implement and utilize these patterns in Rust.

Currying: Partial Application Made Easy

Currying allows you to transform a function that takes multiple arguments into a sequence of functions that each take a single argument. This enables partial application, where you can fix some of the arguments of a function to create a new function with fewer arguments.

Example 1: Currying a Simple Addition Function

```rust
Rust

fn add(x: i32, y: i32) -> i32 {

    x + y

}



fn curried_add(x: i32) -> impl Fn(i32) -> i32 {

    move |y| add(x, y)

}



fn main() {

    let add_five = curried_add(5);

    println!("{}", add_five(3)); // Output: 8

}
```

In this example, curried_add takes one argument x and returns a closure that takes another argument y and adds it to x. This allows you to create specialized functions like add_five that add 5 to their input.

Example 2: Currying a Function with More Arguments

Rust

```rust
fn calculate_area(width: f64, height: f64, depth: f64) -> f64 {

    width * height * depth

}

fn curried_calculate_area(width: f64) -> impl Fn(f64, f64) -> f64 {

    move |height, depth| calculate_area(width, height, depth)

}

fn main() {

                let     calculate_area_with_width_10     =
    curried_calculate_area(10.0);

    println!("{}", calculate_area_with_width_10(5.0, 2.0)); // Output: 100.0

}
```

In this example, curried_calculate_area takes one argument width and returns a closure that takes two more arguments height and depth to calculate the area. This allows you to create specialized functions like calculate_area_with_width_10 that fix the width to 10.0.

Function Composition: Building Complex Logic

Function composition allows you to combine multiple functions to create new functions, building complex logic from simpler, reusable components.

Example 1: Composing Functions to Manipulate Strings

Rust

```rust
fn uppercase(s: String) -> String {

    s.to_uppercase()

}

fn reverse(s: String) -> String {

    s.chars().rev().collect()

}

fn compose<A, B, C, F, G>(f: F, g: G) -> impl Fn(A) -> C

where

    F: Fn(B) -> C,
```

```rust
    G: Fn(A) -> B,
{
    move |x| f(g(x))
}
fn main() {
    let uppercase_and_reverse = compose(reverse, uppercase);
    println!("{}", uppercase_and_reverse("hello".to_string())); // Output: OLLEH
}
```

In this example, compose takes two functions f and g and returns a new function that applies g to its input and then applies f to the result. This allows you to create functions like uppercase_and_reverse that combine the effects of uppercase and reverse.

Example 2: Composing Functions for Data Transformation

Rust

```rust
fn add_one(x: i32) -> i32 {
```

```
    x + 1

}

fn double(x: i32) -> i32 {

    x * 2

}

fn main() {

    let add_one_and_double = compose(double, add_one);

    println!("{}", add_one_and_double(5)); // Output: 12

}
```

In this example, add_one_and_double combines the effects of add_one and double, first adding 1 to the input and then doubling the result.

Memoization: Optimizing for Performance

Memoization is a technique that caches the results of expensive function calls, so that if the function is called again with the same arguments, the cached result is returned instead of recomputing it. This can significantly improve performance for functions with computationally intensive operations.

Example: Memoizing the Fibonacci Function

Rust

```rust
use std::collections::HashMap;


fn fibonacci(n: u64, cache: &mut HashMap<u64, u64>) -> u64 {

    if let Some(&result) = cache.get(&n) {

        return result;

    }

    let result = if n <= 1 {

        n

    } else {

        fibonacci(n - 1, cache) + fibonacci(n - 2, cache)

    };

    cache.insert(n, result);

    result

}


fn main() {

    let mut cache = HashMap::new();
```

```
    println!("{}", fibonacci(10, &mut cache)); // Output: 55

}
```

In this example, fibonacci calculates the nth Fibonacci number. The cache HashMap stores previously computed results. If the result for n is already in the cache, it is returned directly. Otherwise, the result is computed, stored in the cache, and then returned.

By understanding and applying functional design patterns like currying, composition, and memoization, you can enhance the structure, reusability, and efficiency of your Rust code.

Implementing Functional Design Patterns with Closures and Higher-Order Functions

Closures and higher-order functions are powerful tools in Rust that enable the implementation of various functional design patterns, promoting code reusability, modularity, and elegance. Let's explore how closures and higher-order functions can be used to implement common functional design patterns like currying, function composition, and memoization.

Currying with Closures

Currying transforms a function that takes multiple arguments into a sequence of functions that each take a single argument. Closures provide a natural way to implement currying in Rust.

Example:

```rust
Rust

fn add(x: i32, y: i32) -> i32 {

    x + y

}

fn curried_add(x: i32) -> impl Fn(i32) -> i32 {

    move |y| add(x, y)

}

fn main() {

    let add_five = curried_add(5);

    println!("{}", add_five(3)); // Output: 8

}
```

In this example, curried_add takes one argument x and returns a closure that takes another argument y and adds it to x. This allows you to create specialized functions like add_five that add 5 to their input.

Function Composition with Higher-Order Functions

Function composition combines multiple functions to create new functions. Higher-order functions, which take functions as arguments or return functions as results, are essential for implementing function composition.

Example:

Rust

```rust
fn double(x: i32) -> i32 {

    x * 2

}

fn square(x: i32) -> i32 {

    x * x

}

fn compose<A, B, C, F, G>(f: F, g: G) -> impl Fn(A) -> C

where

    F: Fn(B) -> C,

    G: Fn(A) -> B,

{
```

```
    move |x| f(g(x))

}


fn main() {

    let double_then_square = compose(square, double);

    println!("{}", double_then_square(3)); // Output: 36

}
```

In this example, compose takes two functions f and g and returns a new function that applies g to its input and then applies f to the result. This allows you to create functions like double_then_square that combine the effects of double and square.

Memoization with Closures and HashMaps

Memoization caches the results of expensive function calls to avoid redundant computations. Closures and HashMaps can be used together to implement memoization in Rust.

Example:

Rust

```
use std::collections::HashMap;
```

```rust
fn fibonacci(n: u64, cache: &mut HashMap<u64, u64>) -> u64 {
    if let Some(&result) = cache.get(&n) {
        return result;
    }
    let result = if n <= 1 {
        n
    } else {
        fibonacci(n - 1, cache) + fibonacci(n - 2, cache)
    };
    cache.insert(n, result);
    result
}
fn main() {
    let mut cache = HashMap::new();
    println!("{}", fibonacci(10, &mut cache)); // Output: 55
}
```

In this example, fibonacci calculates the nth Fibonacci number. The cache HashMap stores previously computed results. If the result for n is already in the cache, it is returned directly. Otherwise, the result is computed, stored in the cache, and then returned.

Benefits of Using Closures and Higher-Order Functions

- Conciseness: Closures provide a concise syntax for defining anonymous functions, making the code more compact and readable.
- Flexibility: Closures can capture variables from their surrounding scope, allowing them to adapt to different contexts.
- Code Reusability: Higher-order functions promote code reuse by enabling you to abstract common patterns of computation.
- Expressiveness: Closures and higher-order functions make your code more expressive by allowing you to define custom behavior and combine functions in various ways.

By leveraging closures and higher-order functions, you can effectively implement functional design patterns in Rust, enhancing the structure, reusability, and efficiency of your code. These patterns promote a functional programming style, enabling you to write elegant and maintainable programs that are well-suited for various tasks.

Benefits and Trade-offs of Functional Design Patterns: Currying, Composition, and Memoization

Functional design patterns like currying, composition, and memoization offer powerful ways to structure and optimize your code, but they also come with certain trade-offs. Let's explore the benefits and trade-offs of each pattern in detail, helping you make informed decisions about when and how to use them effectively.

Currying

Benefits:

- Code Reusability: Currying allows you to create reusable functions that can be adapted to different contexts by partially applying arguments. This reduces code duplication and promotes modularity.
- Flexibility: It provides flexibility in how you apply arguments to a function, enabling you to fix some arguments while leaving others open for later. This can be useful for creating specialized functions or delaying the evaluation of certain arguments.
- Improved Code Readability: Currying can make your code more readable by breaking down complex functions into smaller, more manageable units. This can improve code comprehension and maintainability.

Trade-offs:

- Increased Complexity: Currying can increase the complexity of your code, especially when dealing with functions with many arguments. The nested structure of curried functions can make it harder to follow the flow of data.
- Performance Overhead: In some cases, currying can introduce a slight performance overhead due to the creation of intermediate closures. However, this overhead is usually negligible in most applications.

Function Composition

Benefits:

- Modularity: Function composition promotes modularity by breaking down complex logic into smaller, reusable functions. This makes your code easier to understand, test, and maintain.
- Code Reusability: It allows you to reuse existing functions in new ways by combining them with other functions. This can save development time and reduce code duplication.
- Improved Code Readability: Function composition can make your code more readable by expressing complex operations as a sequence of simpler operations. This can improve code clarity and comprehension.

Trade-offs:

- Debugging Complexity: Debugging composed functions can be more challenging, as you need to trace the flow of data through multiple functions.
- Type Signatures: The type signatures of composed functions can become complex, especially when composing functions with different types of arguments and return values.

Memoization

Benefits:

- Performance Improvement: Memoization can significantly improve performance for functions with expensive computations by avoiding redundant calculations. This can be crucial for computationally intensive tasks.
- Code Optimization: It can optimize code by reducing the number of times a computationally intensive function is executed. This can lead to significant performance gains in certain scenarios.

Trade-offs:

- Memory Usage: Memoization requires storing cached results, which can increase memory usage. This can be a concern for functions with a large number of possible inputs or very large output values.
- Cache Invalidation: Managing the cache and ensuring its consistency can be challenging, especially in concurrent

environments. You need to carefully consider cache invalidation strategies to avoid stale data.

Summary Table:

Pattern	Benefits	Trade-offs
Currying	Code reusability, flexibility, readability	Increased complexity, potential performance overhead
Function Composition	Modularity, code reusability, readability	Debugging complexity, complex type signatures
Memoization	Performance improvement, code optimization	Increased memory usage, cache invalidation challenges

When to Use Each Pattern:

- Currying: Use currying when you need to create specialized functions by fixing some arguments of a more general function, or when you want to delay the evaluation of certain arguments.

- Function Composition: Use function composition when you want to build complex logic from simpler, reusable functions, or when you want to express a sequence of operations in a more readable way.
- Memoization: Use memoization when you have computationally expensive functions that are called repeatedly with the same arguments, and when the memory usage for caching results is not a concern.

By carefully considering the benefits and trade-offs of each functional design pattern, you can make informed decisions about when and how to use them effectively in your Rust programs. These patterns offer powerful tools for structuring and optimizing your code, promoting a functional programming style and enhancing the elegance and maintainability of your applications.

Building Reusable Functional Components in Rust: A Practical Guide

Functional programming emphasizes modularity and code reusability. In Rust, you can leverage closures, higher-order functions, and functional design patterns to build reusable functional components that can be easily combined and adapted to various contexts. Let's explore some practical examples of how to create reusable functional components in Rust, drawing upon the concepts and techniques we've covered in previous chapters.

Example 1: Reusable Validation Functions

Validation is a common task in many applications, and closures provide a concise and flexible way to define reusable validation functions.

Rust

```
fn validate_length(min_length: usize, max_length: usize) ->
impl Fn(&str) -> bool {
    move |input| input.len() >= min_length && input.len() <=
max_length
}

fn main() {
    let validate_username = validate_length(3, 20);
    let validate_password = validate_length(8, 32);

        println!("Username 'johndoe' is valid: {}",
validate_username("johndoe")); // Output: true
            println!("Password 'short' is valid: {}",
validate_password("short")); // Output: false
}
```

In this example, validate_length is a higher-order function that takes min_length and max_length as arguments and returns a closure that validates the length of a string. This allows you to create reusable validation functions like validate_username and validate_password with different length constraints.

Example 2: Generic Data Transformation with Closures

Closures can be used to define generic data transformation functions that can operate on various types of data.

Rust

```rust
fn map<T, F>(items: Vec<T>, f: F) -> Vec<T>
where
    F: Fn(T) -> T,
{
    items.into_iter().map(f).collect()
}

fn main() {
    let numbers = vec![1, 2, 3, 4, 5];
    let doubled_numbers = map(numbers, |x| x * 2);
    println!("{:?}", doubled_numbers); // Output: [2, 4, 6, 8, 10]

    let strings = vec!["hello", "world"];
    let uppercase_strings = map(strings, |s| s.to_uppercase());
    println!("{:?}", uppercase_strings); // Output: ["HELLO", "WORLD"]
}
```

In this example, map is a generic function that takes a vector of any type T and a closure f that transforms a value of type T into another value of type T. This allows you to use the same map function to transform different types of data, such as numbers or strings.

Example 3: Reusable Logging Component with Closures

Closures can be used to create reusable logging components that can be customized with different logging behaviors.

```rust
Rust

fn log<F>(message: &str, log_function: F)
where
    F: Fn(&str),
{
    log_function(message);
}

fn main() {
    let print_log = |message| println!("Log: {}", message);
    log("Something happened!", print_log);

    let write_log = |message| {
        // ... logic to write the message to a file ...
    };
    log("Something else happened!", write_log);
}
```

In this example, log is a higher-order function that takes a message and a closure log_function as arguments. The closure defines how the message should be logged, allowing you to use different logging mechanisms, such as printing to the console or writing to a file.

Example 4: Reusable Memoization Function

Memoization can be implemented as a reusable function that takes a function and returns a memoized version of that function.

```rust
Rust

use std::collections::HashMap;

fn memoize<A, B, F>(f: F) -> impl Fn(A) -> B
where
    A: Eq + std::hash::Hash + Clone,
    B: Clone,
    F: Fn(A) -> B,
{
    let mut cache = HashMap::new();
    move |arg| {
        if let Some(result) = cache.get(&arg) {
            result.clone()
        } else {
            let result = f(arg.clone());
            cache.insert(arg, result.clone());
            result
        }
```

```
    }
}

fn main() {
    let expensive_calculation = |x: i32| {
        println!("Calculating...");
        x * 2
    };

    let memoized_calculation =
memoize(expensive_calculation);

    println!("{}", memoized_calculation(5)); // Output:
Calculating... 10
    println!("{}", memoized_calculation(5)); // Output: 10
(cached result)
}
```

In this example, memoize takes a function f and returns a memoized version of that function. The memoized version uses a HashMap to cache the results of previous calls to f.

CHAPTER 8

Concurrency and Parallelism with Functional Principles

Rust's Ownership and Borrowing for Safe Concurrency: A Deep Dive

Concurrency in programming, where multiple tasks execute seemingly at the same time, is essential for building high-performance applications that can utilize modern multi-core processors. However, concurrency often introduces challenges like data races and deadlocks, which can lead to unpredictable behavior and crashes. Rust's ownership and borrowing system provides a unique and powerful solution for achieving safe and efficient concurrency without the pitfalls common in other languages. Let's explore how Rust's ownership and borrowing system tackles these challenges, enabling you to write concurrent code with confidence.

Understanding the Challenges of Concurrency

- Data Races: Data races occur when multiple threads access and modify the same memory location simultaneously, leading to unpredictable and inconsistent results.

- Deadlocks: Deadlocks occur when two or more threads are blocked forever, each waiting for the other to release a resource.

These concurrency issues can be difficult to debug and often lead to program crashes or data corruption.

Rust's Ownership and Borrowing: The Foundation for Safe Concurrency

Rust's ownership and borrowing system, as discussed in earlier chapters, provides a set of rules that govern how data is accessed and shared between different parts of your program. These rules, enforced at compile time, prevent data races and deadlocks, ensuring memory safety and thread safety without the need for a garbage collector or runtime checks.

Key Principles:

- Ownership: Every value in Rust has a single owner at any given time. When the owner goes out of scope, the value is automatically dropped.
- Borrowing: Borrowing allows you to temporarily share access to a value without transferring ownership. There are two types of borrows:
  - Immutable Borrows: Shared read-only access.
  - Mutable Borrows: Exclusive write access.

The Rules:

- You can have either one mutable borrow or multiple immutable borrows, but not both at the same time.
- Borrows must always be valid. The compiler ensures that a borrow cannot outlive the owner of the borrowed value.

How Ownership and Borrowing Prevent Concurrency Issues

- Data Races: The borrowing rules prevent data races by ensuring that only one thread can mutably access a piece of data at a time. If multiple threads need to access the same data, they can do so immutably, preventing any modifications that could lead to inconsistencies.
- Deadlocks: The ownership system prevents deadlocks by ensuring that resources are properly released when they are no longer needed. When a value goes out of scope, its associated resources are automatically deallocated, preventing them from being held indefinitely by a thread.

Concurrency Primitives in Rust

Rust provides several concurrency primitives that leverage the ownership and borrowing system to ensure safe and efficient concurrency:

- Threads: Threads allow you to execute multiple tasks concurrently. Rust's ownership and borrowing rules ensure that data shared between threads is accessed safely.
- Channels: Channels provide a way for threads to communicate and share data safely. They allow you to send values between threads without the risk of data races.
- Mutexes: Mutexes provide mutual exclusion, allowing only one thread to access a shared resource at a time. Rust's ownership and borrowing system ensures that mutexes are used correctly and prevent deadlocks.
- Atomics: Atomics provide lock-free data structures that can be safely accessed and modified by multiple threads concurrently.

Example: Safe Data Sharing with Channels

Rust

```
use std::sync::mpsc;
use std::thread;

fn main() {
  let (sender, receiver) = mpsc::channel();

  thread::spawn(move || {
    let message = String::from("Hello from thread!");
    sender.send(message).unwrap();
  });
```

```rust
    let received_message = receiver.recv().unwrap();
    println!("{}", received_message); // Output: Hello from thread!
}
```

In this example, a channel is used to safely send a message from one thread to another. The ownership of the message is transferred through the channel, preventing any data races.

Benefits of Rust's Approach to Concurrency

- Safety: The ownership and borrowing system prevents data races and deadlocks at compile time, ensuring memory safety and thread safety without runtime overhead.
- Efficiency: Rust's concurrency primitives are designed to be efficient, minimizing the overhead of synchronization and communication between threads.
- Clarity: The explicit ownership and borrowing rules make it easier to reason about concurrent code and understand how data is shared between threads.

Table Summarizing Concurrency Primitives

Primitive	Description

Threads	Execute multiple tasks concurrently
Channels	Communicate and share data safely between threads
Mutexes	Provide mutual exclusion for shared resources
Atomics	Offer lock-free data structures for concurrent access

RUST'S CONCURRENCY IN ACTION: Examples and Code

In previous discussions, we explored how Rust's ownership and borrowing system ensures safe and efficient concurrency. Now, let's solidify your understanding with practical examples and code snippets, demonstrating how to use concurrency primitives like threads and channels effectively.

Example 1: Simple Thread Creation

```rust
Rust

use std::thread;


fn main() {
```

```
thread::spawn(|| {

    println!("Hello from a thread!");

});

}
```

This code demonstrates basic thread creation. The thread::spawn function creates a new thread that executes the provided closure.

Example 2: Threads with Data Sharing (Move Semantics)

Rust

```
use std::thread;

fn main() {

    let message = String::from("Hello from main thread!");

    thread::spawn(move || {

        println!("{}", message); // Ownership of message is moved to the thread

    });

}
```

Here, the message variable is moved into the thread's closure, ensuring safe access to the data within the thread.

Example 3: Channels for Communication

Rust

```
use std::sync::mpsc;

use std::thread;

fn main() {

    let (sender, receiver) = mpsc::channel();

    thread::spawn(move || {

        let message = String::from("Hello from thread!");

        sender.send(message).unwrap();

    });

    let received_message = receiver.recv().unwrap();

        println!("{}", received_message); // Output: Hello from
thread!

}
```

This example demonstrates how channels facilitate safe communication between threads. The sender sends a message through the channel, and the receiver receives it.

Example 4: Shared State with Mutexes

Rust

```rust
use std::sync::{Arc, Mutex};

use std::thread;


fn main() {

    let counter = Arc::new(Mutex::new(0));

    let mut handles = vec!;


    for _ in 0..10 {

        let counter = Arc::clone(&counter);

        let handle = thread::spawn(move || {

            let mut num = counter.lock().unwrap();

            *num += 1;

        });

        handles.push(handle);

    }

    for handle in handles {
```

```rust
    handle.join().unwrap();

}
```

```rust
    println!("Result: {}", *counter.lock().unwrap()); // Output:
Result: 10

}
```

This example demonstrates how to safely share mutable state between threads using a mutex. The Arc provides a thread-safe shared ownership of the mutex, and the Mutex ensures that only one thread can access the counter at a time.

Example 5: Parallel Iteration with Rayon

Rust

```rust
use rayon::prelude::*;


fn main() {

    let numbers = vec![1, 2, 3, 4, 5];


    let sum: i32 = numbers

        .par_iter() // Create a parallel iterator
```

```
    .map(|x| x * 2)

    .sum();


    println!("Sum: {}", sum); // Output: Sum: 30

}
```

This example demonstrates how to use the rayon crate for parallel iteration. The par_iter method creates a parallel iterator that can process the elements of the vector concurrently, potentially improving performance.

These examples showcase the power and flexibility of Rust's concurrency primitives. By leveraging the ownership and borrowing system, you can write concurrent code that is safe, efficient, and easy to reason about. Remember, these primitives are designed to prevent common concurrency pitfalls like data races and deadlocks, enabling you to build robust and high-performance applications.

THREADS AND CHANNELS: Communicating with Elegance

In the world of concurrent programming, where multiple threads execute independently, communication and data sharing between threads become crucial for coordinating their activities and achieving desired outcomes. Rust provides a powerful mechanism for inter-thread communication using channels, which act as conduits for safely passing messages between threads. Let's explore how threads and channels work together, enabling you to write elegant and efficient concurrent programs.

Threads: The Actors of Concurrency

Threads are independent units of execution within a program. They allow you to perform multiple tasks concurrently, potentially utilizing multiple CPU cores for improved performance. Each thread has its own stack and local variables, but they can share access to the same memory space, which can lead to data races if not managed carefully.

Channels: The Communication Bridge

Channels provide a safe and structured way for threads to communicate and share data. A channel consists of two endpoints: a sender and a receiver. The sender can send messages into the channel, while the receiver can receive messages from the channel. This unidirectional flow of data helps prevent data races and ensures that messages are delivered in an orderly manner.

Creating Channels

In Rust, you can create a channel using the mpsc::channel() function from the std::sync::mpsc module. This function returns a tuple containing the sender and receiver endpoints.

Rust

```rust
use std::sync::mpsc;

fn main() {

    let (sender, receiver) = mpsc::channel();

    // ... use the sender and receiver to communicate between threads ...

}
```

Sending Messages

The sender endpoint provides a send() method that allows you to send a message into the channel. The send() method takes ownership of the message and transfers it to the receiving thread.

Rust

```rust
sender.send(message).unwrap();
```

Receiving Messages

The receiver endpoint provides a recv() method that allows you to receive a message from the channel. The recv() method blocks until a message is available, ensuring that the receiving thread waits for the message to be sent before proceeding.

```rust
let received_message = receiver.recv().unwrap();
```

Example: Passing Messages Between Threads

Let's consider a scenario where you have two threads: a producer thread that generates data and a consumer thread that processes the data. You can use a channel to pass the data from the producer to the consumer.

Rust

```rust
use std::sync::mpsc;

use std::thread;


fn main() {

    let (sender, receiver) = mpsc::channel();


    thread::spawn(move || {

        let data = vec![1, 2, 3, 4, 5];

        for value in data {
```

```
        sender.send(value).unwrap();

    }

});


for received_value in receiver {

    println!("Received: {}", received_value);

}

}
```

In this example, the producer thread generates a vector of numbers and sends each number through the channel. The consumer thread receives the numbers from the channel and prints them to the console.

Benefits of Using Channels

- Safe Data Sharing: Channels ensure safe data sharing between threads by transferring ownership of the messages, preventing data races and ensuring data integrity.
- Synchronization: Channels provide a built-in synchronization mechanism, ensuring that the receiving thread waits for the message to be sent before

proceeding, preventing race conditions and ensuring proper ordering of operations.

- Flexibility: Channels can be used to pass various types of data between threads, including primitive types, structs, enums, and even closures.
- Modularity: Channels promote modularity by decoupling the sending and receiving threads, allowing them to operate independently without direct dependencies.

By leveraging threads and channels, you can write concurrent programs that are safe, efficient, and elegant. Channels provide a powerful mechanism for inter-thread communication, enabling you to coordinate the activities of multiple threads and build robust and responsive applications. Remember, channels are a valuable tool in your concurrency toolkit, empowering you to embrace the full potential of parallel processing in Rust.

Parallel Processing with Iterators: Embracing par_iter for Functional Parallelism

In the world of high-performance computing, parallel processing plays a crucial role in utilizing the full potential of modern multi-core processors. Rust, with its focus on performance and safety, offers powerful tools for parallel processing, including the par_iter method for iterators. This method, provided by the rayon crate, enables you to process elements of an iterator in parallel, potentially significantly reducing computation time. Let's explore par_iter and its functional approach to parallel processing, understanding how it can enhance the efficiency of your Rust programs.

The rayon Crate: Simplifying Parallelism

The rayon crate provides a user-friendly and safe way to introduce parallelism into your Rust code. It offers a functional approach to parallelism, allowing you to parallelize operations on iterators without having to manage threads or synchronization primitives manually.

par_iter: The Parallel Iterator

The par_iter method, available on types that implement the IntoParallelIterator trait, creates a parallel iterator that can process elements concurrently. This allows you to apply operations like map, filter, and fold in parallel, distributing the workload across multiple CPU cores.

Example: Parallel Map

Rust

```rust
use rayon::prelude::*;

fn main() {
    let numbers = vec![1, 2, 3, 4, 5];

    let doubled_numbers: Vec<i32> = numbers
        .par_iter()
        .map(|x| x * 2)
```

```
    .collect();

    println!("{:?}", doubled_numbers); // Output: [2, 4, 6, 8, 10]
(order may vary)
}
```

In this example, par_iter creates a parallel iterator over the numbers vector. The map operation is then applied to each element in parallel, potentially utilizing multiple cores for faster execution.

Example: Parallel Filter

Rust

```
use rayon::prelude::*;

fn main() {
    let numbers = vec![1, 2, 3, 4, 5];

    let even_numbers: Vec<i32> = numbers
        .par_iter()
        .filter(|x| *x % 2 == 0)
        .collect();
```

```
    println!("{:?}", even_numbers); // Output: [2, 4] (order may
vary)
}
```

Here, par_iter and filter are used to select even numbers from
the vector in parallel.

Example: Parallel Fold (Reduce)

Rust

```
use rayon::prelude::*;

fn main() {
    let numbers = vec![1, 2, 3, 4, 5];

    let sum: i32 = numbers
        .par_iter()
        .sum();

    println!("{}", sum); // Output: 15
}
```

In this example, par_iter and sum are used to calculate the sum
of the numbers in parallel.

Important Considerations

- Data Independence: Parallel processing with par_iter is most effective when the operations on each element are independent of each other. If the operations have dependencies, you might need to use other concurrency primitives like channels or mutexes to manage shared state.
- Overhead: There is some overhead associated with creating and managing threads for parallel processing. For small datasets or simple operations, the overhead might outweigh the benefits of parallelism.
- Order of Results: The order of results in parallel iterators might not be the same as the original order of elements. If the order is important, you might need to use collect to gather the results into a vector and then sort it.

PARALLEL ITERATORS IN RUST: A Hands-On Exploration with par_iter

In our previous discussion, we introduced the concept of parallel iterators and the par_iter method from the rayon crate. Now, let's delve deeper into this powerful tool with practical examples and code snippets, showcasing how you can leverage parallel iterators to boost the performance of your Rust programs.

Example 1: Parallel Map with par_iter

The map operation, commonly used to transform elements of an iterator, can be easily parallelized using par_iter. This allows you to apply a transformation to each element concurrently, potentially reducing the overall computation time.

```rust
use rayon::prelude::*;

fn main() {

    let numbers = vec![1, 2, 3, 4, 5];

    let doubled_numbers: Vec<i32> = numbers

        .par_iter() // Create a parallel iterator

        .map(|x| {

                println!("Doubling {} on thread {:?}", x,
thread::current().id());

            x * 2

        })

        .collect();

    println!("{:?}", doubled_numbers); // Output: [2, 4, 6, 8, 10]
(order may vary)
```

}

In this example, par_iter creates a parallel iterator over the numbers vector. The map operation then doubles each element concurrently, potentially utilizing multiple CPU cores. The println! statement inside the map closure demonstrates that the doubling operations can occur on different threads.

Example 2: Parallel Filter with par_iter

The filter operation, used to select elements from an iterator based on a predicate, can also be parallelized using par_iter. This allows you to filter elements concurrently, potentially speeding up the filtering process.

Rust

```
use rayon::prelude::*;

fn main() {

    let numbers = vec![1, 2, 3, 4, 5];

    let even_numbers: Vec<i32> = numbers

        .par_iter() // Create a parallel iterator

        .filter(|x| {
```

```
            println!("Filtering {} on thread {:?}", x,
thread::current().id());

    *x % 2 == 0

})

.collect();

println!("{:?}", even_numbers); // Output: [2, 4] (order may
vary)

}
```

In this example, par_iter creates a parallel iterator, and the filter operation selects only the even numbers concurrently. The println! statement inside the filter closure shows that the filtering operations can occur on different threads.

Example 3: Parallel Fold (Reduce) with par_iter

The fold operation, also known as reduce, combines the elements of an iterator into a single value. Using par_iter, you can perform this reduction in parallel, potentially improving performance for large datasets.

Rust

```
use rayon::prelude::*;
```

```rust
fn main() {

    let numbers = vec![1, 2, 3, 4, 5];

    let sum: i32 = numbers

        .par_iter() // Create a parallel iterator

        .sum();

    println!("{}", sum); // Output: 15

}
```

In this example, par_iter creates a parallel iterator, and the sum operation calculates the sum of the numbers concurrently.

Important Considerations

- Data Independence: Parallel processing with par_iter is most effective when the operations on each element are independent of each other. If the operations have dependencies, you might need to use other concurrency primitives like channels or mutexes to manage shared state.
- Overhead: There is some overhead associated with creating and managing threads for parallel processing.

For small datasets or simple operations, the overhead might outweigh the benefits of parallelism.

- Order of Results: The order of results in parallel iterators might not be the same as the original order of elements. If the order is important, you might need to use collect to gather the results into a vector and then sort it.

Benefits of par_iter

- Ease of Use: par_iter provides a simple and functional way to introduce parallelism into your code without having to manage threads or synchronization manually.
- Performance Improvement: For computationally intensive tasks with independent operations, par_iter can significantly improve performance by utilizing multiple CPU cores.
- Integration with Iterators: par_iter integrates seamlessly with existing iterator adapters, allowing you to combine parallel processing with other data transformations.

By leveraging par_iter and the rayon crate, you can embrace functional parallelism in Rust, writing efficient and concurrent code that can take full advantage of modern multi-core processors. Remember, par_iter is a valuable tool in your concurrency toolkit, empowering you to explore the world of parallel processing with ease and safety.

Building Concurrent Data Pipelines and Performing Parallel Computations in Rust

Concurrency in Rust, empowered by its ownership and borrowing system, allows you to build efficient and safe data pipelines and perform parallel computations, maximizing the utilization of modern multi-core processors. Let's explore these concepts in detail, drawing upon the concurrency primitives and functional programming techniques we've covered in previous chapters.

Building Concurrent Data Pipelines

Data pipelines are a series of stages where data is processed sequentially, with each stage performing a specific transformation or computation. Concurrency can significantly enhance the efficiency of data pipelines by allowing different stages to operate concurrently, potentially reducing the overall processing time.

Example: Image Processing Pipeline

Imagine you have a pipeline for processing images, where each stage performs a different operation, such as resizing, filtering, and compression. You can use threads and channels to parallelize these stages, allowing them to operate concurrently.

Rust

```
use std::sync::mpsc;
```

```rust
use std::thread;

// Define a struct to represent an image
struct Image {
    // ... image data ...
}

fn main() {
    let (sender1, receiver1) = mpsc::channel();
    let (sender2, receiver2) = mpsc::channel();

    // Stage 1: Resize images
    thread::spawn(move || {
        for image in receiver1 {
            let resized_image = resize_image(image);
            sender2.send(resized_image).unwrap();
        }
    });

    // Stage 2: Apply filters
    thread::spawn(move || {
        for image in receiver2 {
            let filtered_image = apply_filters(image);
            // ... further processing or storage ...
        }
    });

    // Send images to the pipeline
    let images = vec![
        Image { /* ... */ },
```

```rust
        Image { /* ... */ },
        Image { /* ... */ },
    ];
    for image in images {
        sender1.send(image).unwrap();
    }
}

fn resize_image(image: Image) -> Image {
    // ... logic to resize the image ...
    image
}

fn apply_filters(image: Image) -> Image {
    // ... logic to apply filters to the image ...
    image
}
```

In this example, two threads are used to create a concurrent pipeline. The first thread resizes the images and sends them to the second thread through a channel. The second thread applies filters to the resized images. This allows the resizing and filtering operations to occur concurrently, potentially reducing the overall processing time.

Performing Parallel Computations

Parallel computations involve breaking down a large computational task into smaller subtasks that can be executed concurrently, combining the results to produce the final output. Rust's concurrency primitives and functional programming features provide a powerful framework for performing parallel computations.

Example: Calculating the Mandelbrot Set

The Mandelbrot set is a famous fractal that requires significant computation to generate. You can parallelize the computation of the Mandelbrot set by dividing the image into smaller regions and processing each region concurrently.

Rust

```rust
use rayon::prelude::*;

fn calculate_mandelbrot(x: f64, y: f64, max_iterations: usize) -> usize {
    // ... logic to calculate the Mandelbrot value for a given point
    ...
    // This is a computationally intensive operation
}

fn main() {
    let width = 1000;
    let height = 1000;
    let max_iterations = 1000;

    let mut image = vec![vec![0; width]; height];

    image
```

```
    .par_iter_mut()
    .enumerate()
    .for_each(|(y, row)| {
       row.par_iter_mut()
          .enumerate()
          .for_each(|(x, pixel)| {
             let x_coord = (x as f64 - width as f64 / 2.0) /
(width as f64 / 4.0);
             let y_coord = (y as f64 - height as f64 / 2.0) /
(height as f64 / 4.0);
             *pixel = calculate_mandelbrot(x_coord, y_coord,
max_iterations);
          });
    });

    // ... use the image data to render the Mandelbrot set ...
}
```

In this example, par_iter_mut is used to create parallel iterators over the rows and pixels of the image. The calculate_mandelbrot function, which is computationally intensive, is applied to each pixel in parallel, potentially significantly reducing the overall computation time.

Benefits of Concurrent Data Pipelines and Parallel Computations

- Performance Improvement: Concurrency can significantly improve performance by utilizing multiple

CPU cores, reducing the overall processing time for computationally intensive tasks.

- Responsiveness: Concurrent data pipelines can improve the responsiveness of applications by allowing different stages to operate independently, preventing blocking and ensuring smooth data flow.

- Resource Utilization: Parallel computations can efficiently utilize available resources, maximizing the use of multi-core processors and potentially reducing energy consumption.

By leveraging Rust's concurrency primitives and functional programming techniques, you can build efficient and safe concurrent data pipelines and perform parallel computations, unlocking the full potential of modern hardware and enhancing the performance of your applications. Remember, concurrency is a powerful tool in your Rust development arsenal, enabling you to write high-performance and responsive programs that can tackle complex computational challenges.

CHAPTER 9:

Putting It All Together: Building a Functional Application

Building a Concurrent URL Fetcher: A Practical Application of Functional Programming in Rust

Throughout this book, we've explored various functional programming concepts and techniques in Rust, including closures, iterators, higher-order functions, error handling, and concurrency. Now, let's put these concepts into practice by building a small application that fetches data from multiple URLs concurrently, showcasing the power and elegance of functional programming in a real-world scenario.

Project Overview

Our application will be a concurrent URL fetcher that takes a list of URLs as input and fetches the content of each URL concurrently using threads. The fetched data will then be processed and aggregated, demonstrating the use of functional programming principles for data manipulation and transformation.

Project Structure

We'll structure our project using a modular approach, separating the different functionalities into separate functions and modules. This promotes code organization and reusability.[1]

```
src/
├── main.rs        // Main application logic
├── fetcher.rs     // URL fetching functionality
└── processor.rs   // Data processing and aggregation
```

Dependencies

We'll use the following external crates for our project:

- reqwest: For making HTTP requests.
- rayon: For parallel processing.
- error-chain: For streamlined error handling.

You can add these dependencies to your Cargo.toml file:

Ini, TOML

```
[dependencies]
reqwest = "0.11"
rayon = "1.5"
error-chain = "0.12"
```

Error Handling

We'll use the error-chain crate to define our own error types and streamline error handling throughout the application.

Rust

```rust
// In error.rs
use error_chain::error_chain;

error_chain! {
    foreign_links {
        Reqwest(reqwest::Error);
        Io(std::io::Error);
    }
}
```

URL Fetching

The fetcher.rs module will contain the functionality for fetching data from URLs concurrently.

Rust

```rust
// In fetcher.rs
use crate::errors::*;
use reqwest;
use rayon::prelude::*;

pub async fn fetch_urls(urls: Vec<&str>) -> Result<Vec<String>> {
    urls.par_iter()
```

```
    .map(|url| -> Result<String> {
        let response = reqwest::get(url).await?;
        let body = response.text().await?;
        Ok(body)
    })
    .collect()
}
```

The fetch_urls function takes a vector of URLs and returns a Result containing a vector of fetched data. It uses par_iter from the rayon crate to process the URLs concurrently, potentially improving performance. The ? operator is used to propagate any errors that occur during the fetching process.

Data Processing

The processor.rs module will contain the functionality for processing and aggregating the fetched data.

Rust

```
// In processor.rs
pub fn process_data(data: Vec<String>) -> String {
    // ... logic to process and aggregate the data ...
    data.join("\n")
}
```

The process_data function takes a vector of strings and returns a single string containing the processed and aggregated data. In this example, it simply joins the strings with newlines.

Main Application Logic

The main.rs file will contain the main application logic, orchestrating the URL fetching and data processing.

Rust

```
// In main.rs
use crate::errors::*;
use crate::fetcher;
use crate::processor;

#[tokio::main]
async fn main() -> Result<()> {
    let urls = vec![
        "https://example.com/data1",
        "https://example.com/data2",
        "https://example.com/data3",
    ];

    let data = fetcher::fetch_urls(urls).await?;
    let processed_data = processor::process_data(data);

    println!("{}", processed_data);

    Ok(())
}
```

The main function defines the list of URLs to fetch, calls the fetch_urls function to fetch the data concurrently, and then calls the process_data function to process and aggregate the fetched data. The final result is printed to the console.

Running the Application

You can run the application using cargo run. It will fetch the data from the specified URLs concurrently, process the data, and print the final result to the console.

This comprehensive example demonstrates how to build a small application using various functional programming concepts and techniques in Rust. By leveraging closures, iterators, higher-order functions, error handling, and concurrency, you can create elegant, efficient, and robust applications that can tackle real-world challenges. This project showcases the power and expressiveness of functional programming in Rust, enabling you to write concurrent and maintainable code that can take full advantage of modern hardware and software architectures.

Best Practices for Functional Programming in Rust

Functional programming in Rust offers a powerful paradigm for writing clean, maintainable, and efficient code. By adhering to best practices, you can maximize the benefits of this approach and create robust applications that are easy to reason about and adapt. Let's explore some key best practices for functional programming in Rust, drawing upon the concepts and techniques we've covered throughout this book.

Immutability: Embrace the Power of Unchanging Data

Immutability is a cornerstone of functional programming, promoting predictability, thread safety, and easier debugging. In Rust, strive to use immutable data structures and variables whenever possible. This reduces the risk of unintended side effects and makes your code easier to reason about.

- Use const for compile-time constants: For values that are known at compile time, use the const keyword to declare them as immutable constants.
- Favor let over let mut: When declaring variables, use let by default to create immutable bindings. Only use let mut when you explicitly need to modify the variable's value.
- Prefer immutable data structures: When working with collections, use immutable methods like iter() and map() to transform data without modifying the original collection.

Pure Functions: Predictability and Testability

Pure functions are functions that have no side effects and always produce the same output for the same input. They are essential for writing reliable and testable functional code.

- Minimize side effects: Strive to write functions that do not modify any external state or have any observable side effects. This makes your functions more predictable and easier to test.

- Favor immutability within functions: When working with data within a function, prefer immutable borrows and transformations to avoid modifying the original data.
- Use pure functions for data transformations: When transforming data, use pure functions to ensure that the transformations are predictable and do not have any unintended consequences.

Higher-Order Functions: Abstraction and Reusability

Higher-order functions, which take functions as arguments or return functions as results, enable powerful abstractions and promote code reusability.

- Use closures for custom behavior: Closures provide a concise and flexible way to define anonymous functions that can capture variables from their surrounding scope. Use closures to customize the behavior of higher-order functions.
- Abstract common patterns: Identify common patterns in your code and abstract them into reusable higher-order functions. This can reduce code duplication and improve code organization.
- Compose functions for complex logic: Use function composition to combine simpler functions into more complex ones, promoting modularity and code readability.

Error Handling: Explicit and Functional

Error handling in Rust is explicit and functional, using the Result type and its associated combinators.

- Use Result for fallible operations: When a function might fail, use the Result type to explicitly represent the possibility of an error.
- Handle errors gracefully: Use pattern matching or combinators to handle both the Ok and Err cases of a Result, providing informative feedback to the user.
- Propagate errors appropriately: Use the ? operator to propagate errors up the call stack or use combinators like and_then to chain fallible operations.

Concurrency: Safety and Efficiency

Rust's ownership and borrowing system ensures safe and efficient concurrency.

- Use threads for independent tasks: Use threads to execute independent tasks concurrently, potentially utilizing multiple CPU cores for improved performance.
- Use channels for communication: Use channels to safely communicate and share data between threads, preventing data races and ensuring data integrity.
- Use mutexes for shared state: Use mutexes to protect shared data from concurrent access, ensuring data consistency and preventing data corruption.
- Use parallel iterators for parallel processing: Use parallel iterators from the rayon crate to process

elements of an iterator concurrently, potentially improving performance for computationally intensive tasks.

Additional Best Practices

- Keep functions short and focused: Strive to write functions that perform a single, well-defined task. This improves code readability and maintainability.
- Use meaningful names: Choose descriptive names for functions, variables, and data structures to make your code easier to understand.
- Write clear and concise code: Avoid unnecessary complexity and strive for code that is easy to read and follow.
- Test your code thoroughly: Write unit tests to ensure that your functions behave as expected and to prevent regressions when making changes to your code.

By following these best practices, you can write functional code in Rust that is safe, efficient, and maintainable. Functional programming provides a powerful paradigm for building robust and scalable applications, and by adhering to these principles, you can maximize the benefits of this approach and create high-quality software that is a joy to work with.

Where to Go from Here: Continuing Your Functional Journey in Rust

Congratulations on reaching the end of this book! You've embarked on a journey through the world of functional programming in Rust, exploring concepts like closures, iterators, higher-order functions, error handling, and concurrency. You've learned how to apply these concepts to build elegant, efficient, and robust applications, embracing the power and expressiveness of functional programming paradigms. But your journey doesn't end here. The world of functional programming is vast and ever-evolving, and there's always more to learn and explore.

Deepening Your Understanding

- Explore Advanced Functional Concepts: Delve deeper into advanced functional programming concepts like monads, functors, and applicative functors. These concepts provide powerful abstractions for handling side effects, composing functions, and working with data in a structured way.
- Study Functional Programming Libraries: Rust offers a rich ecosystem of libraries that provide functional programming tools and abstractions. Explore libraries like itertools, either, and futures to expand your functional programming toolkit.
- Read Functional Programming Books and Articles: There are numerous books and articles available that explore functional programming concepts and techniques in depth. Expand your knowledge by reading

works by renowned functional programming experts and practitioners.

Expanding Your Rust Skills

- Master the Rust Language: Continue to deepen your understanding of the Rust language itself, exploring its advanced features like macros, traits, and generics. These features can further enhance your ability to write expressive and reusable functional code.
- Contribute to Open-Source Projects: Contribute to open-source Rust projects that utilize functional programming principles. This will give you practical experience and expose you to different coding styles and approaches.
- Engage with the Rust Community: Join the vibrant Rust community, participate in online forums and discussions, and attend conferences and meetups. This will help you stay up-to-date with the latest developments in the Rust ecosystem and connect with other passionate Rustaceans.

Applying Functional Programming

- Build Real-World Applications: Apply your functional programming skills to build real-world applications, tackling challenges in various domains like web development, data science, and systems programming.

- Explore Functional Programming Paradigms: Experiment with different functional programming paradigms like pure functional programming, reactive programming, and logic programming. Each paradigm offers unique perspectives and tools for solving different types of problems.
- Share Your Knowledge: Share your functional programming knowledge and experience with others through blog posts, articles, or presentations. This will help spread the adoption of functional programming and contribute to the growth of the Rust community.

A Final Note

As you continue your functional programming journey in Rust, remember to embrace the core principles of immutability, pure functions, and higher-order functions. These principles will guide you in writing clean, maintainable, and efficient code that is a joy to work with. Keep learning, keep experimenting, and keep contributing to the vibrant world of functional programming in Rust. The future of programming is functional, and with Rust, you're well-equipped to be a part of it.

www.ingramcontent.com/pod-product-compliance
Lightning Source LLC
LaVergne TN
LVHW081521050326
832903LV00025B/1574